You Are More Than Magic

The Black and Brown Girls' Guide to Finding Your Voice

MINDA HARTS

Dial Books

Dial Books
An imprint of Penguin Random House LLC, New York

First published in the United States of America by Dial Books,
an imprint of Penguin Random House LLC, 2022

Text copyright © 2022 by Minda Harts

Foreword copyright © 2022 by Valeisha Butterfield Jones

Dial & colophon are registered trademarks of Penguin Random House LLC.

Visit us online at penguinrandomhouse.com.

Library of Congress Cataloging-in-Publication Data is available.

Printed in the United States of America

ISBN 9780593326619

1 3 5 7 9 10 8 6 4 2

LSCH

Design by Cerise Steel
Text set in Macklin Text

"Black girl stories aren't just for Black girls,
they're for everybody."—Marley Dias

To My Mentors, Teachers, and Friends—
thank you for being part of my Black girl joy.

Contents

Foreword

Success is a journey filled with ups and downs. As you grow into a young adult, there are times that the world and many of your peers will celebrate your accomplishments, often calling them magic. To someone watching, the culmination of your education, work experiences, and career progression will be awe-inspiring and even appear, at times, like a superpower or some form of magic.

The reality is that it is *far* from magic. The lack of representation of women, people of color, and underrepresented communities in leadership positions has left an immense void of creativity, innovation, and diverse perspectives required for any business to thrive. The business imperative for diverse leadership has reached an all-time high, requiring companies to evaluate and prioritize inclusive hiring practices and leadership.

While data supports the lack of representation, we also know firsthand the demands of being the "first." From First Lady Michelle Obama to Vice President Kamala Harris to the only two Black women CEO's of Fortune 500 companies at the time of this book's writing, Rosalind Brewer (Walgreens) and Thasunda Brown Duckett (TIAA), the notion that magic has anything to do with their success is a major understatement.

Success may look magical, but it is not.

Success requires grit, fierce intellect, and many sacrifices, both seen and unseen. Countless hours, brave decisions, and bold pivots along the way that define your character and eventually become the layers of success that you will undoubtedly build up and earn over time. There is no blueprint for success. As women and young adults continue to break corporate barriers and glass ceilings, we learn year after year the tremendous sacrifices that are made.

Many of those sacrifices include pay disparities, health challenges, lack of time spent nurturing loving relationships with close family members and friends, or the inability to care for your parents or grandparents as they grow older. Success is more than a notion and requires a close network of family and friends and the ability to give yourself grace and space, when needed.

The combination of a lack of representation coupled with the at times grueling reality that as a young adult you may have to work harder, smarter, faster, and more strategically than your counterparts to disrupt biases in the workplace and society are why Minda Harts challenges us to redefine the notion of magic.

Minda brings to life the realities of being a young person with big dreams, and highlights the true character and work required to make them a reality. *You Are More Than Magic* is a detailed account of turning your purpose into a successful career path and how to mentally reset your expectations so that you're prepared to fully manifest your dreams.

—Valeisha Butterfield Jones, co-president
of The Recording Academy

CHAPTER 1

The Big Shake-Up

When I was eleven years old, I felt like I had no cares in the world.

I was living in sunny Southern California, and at the time the older of two kids; my youngest brother wasn't born yet. I spent weekends playing with all my cousins and shopping at "Penny's" with my grandmother. I didn't think my life could get any better.

I had the pleasure of growing up with my mother's side of the family (my mom is one of five sisters). I had never pictured my life without them a short car ride away. At the time, I had so many amazing Black women surrounding me with love, like my grandmother and great-grandmother, and my grandmother's sister, my aunt Neicy. All of these amazing women made me feel like anything was possible for me.

The sense of belonging I felt at that age is something I wish I could bottle up and give to every young Black girl I meet. It's a feeling I didn't know that I would need to hold tightly to later in my life.

. . .

When I least expected it, my dad told us we were moving to Illinois, where he was going to start a church in the small town where he grew up.

How could he?! We were so close to our family in California, and I had never lived anywhere else. I mean—people dream about moving to California; I had never heard of a mass exodus to Illinois! I lived two doors down from one of my aunts, and I could walk to her house at will. I was on a personal campaign to get her to stop smoking cigarettes—she was down to a few cigarettes a day—I couldn't leave now, we were starting to make real progress!

Now, you might be thinking, "Minda, what does your family leaving California have to do with this book?" And I am so glad you asked that question! That family move changed my life forever. If it had not been for that move from California to Illinois, I probably wouldn't have written this book.

When I moved to that small, majority white town in rural Illinois, it was the first time I remember experiencing racism. It was the first time that I felt being a Black girl wasn't beautiful. And, it was the first time I questioned whether I belonged. The lessons and stories that I will share with you in this book are about some of the hard lessons and ugly truths I learned as a Black girl in a small, white town that only trial and error could teach me.

If I'd had a book like this one back then, I might have loved the skin I'm in so much earlier in my life. Back then, I was going through the angst of being a teenager and feeling isolated, like many teenagers probably feel, regardless of race. But not all teenagers will experience being one of the only Black girls in a class full of white kids, nor will every teenager be called racial slurs. And not every girl will grow up in a country that treats people like her as second-class citizens because they are Black or brown. If I had a book like *You Are More Than Magic* when I was growing up, I might have been able to see my own worth way before I became an adult.

I don't want you to move through life not knowing how amazing you are, just the way you are. Other people don't get to dictate how you use your voice and how you choose to show up in this world as a young girl living in her color—living in your beautiful Black or brown skin. You need to know right now: You are more than magic at this very moment in time.

I Am Not Dora the Explorer

Before moving to Illinois, I lived in an area of California called the Inland Empire, which was racially diverse.

Representation was all around me: My community included Mexican kids, Native American kids, biracial kids, kids from all sorts of backgrounds. And I was never the only girl of color in my classroom. I was exposed to so many cultures living in our community, and I didn't know anything different from diversity. At eleven, I thought the rest of the world was experiencing the same America as I was.

So, moving to a town that was far from diverse felt like moving to an entirely new country. When we finally got settled in Illinois, our family stuck out like a sore thumb. The town was predominately white. The second-largest group was Latinx, but they were still a small percentage of the population. I was thrust into a new experience of being "the only one." I was the only Black student or student of color in my classes and on my block.

Quick Q's: **Have you ever been the only one? How did that make you feel?**

For the first time in my life, I was the only Black girl. I had no idea how much being the only one would dictate how some of my teachers would treat me, or who wanted to date me, or the words my white friends would use because they heard them in a rap song. I quickly learned the beauty standards of rural white America, and they didn't include a "Black is beautiful" campaign. (Now, don't get me wrong—everybody wanted to be my friend. I was the new shiny Black girl—and it was "cool" for them to finally have a Black friend.)

When we arrived, we moved into a small, one-bedroom apartment that happened to place my family at one of the most affluent schools in town. Almost 99 percent of the students were white, and their parents or guardians were doctors, nurses, and teachers. My parents did not have those types of jobs, at the time, and we didn't have that type of money. And with all these changes I was experiencing, it was the first time I felt ashamed of where we lived and what we didn't have.

Before we moved to Illinois, I had no idea we were what some might consider "working poor." In this new place, imposter syndrome started to creep in. And if you don't know what imposter syndrome is—I will tell you more about it in later chapters.

Back in the day, we didn't have a fancy name to call it, but I would soon understand the shame associated with being in the free lunch line when my friends were not. Or going on my eighth-grade graduation trip to Six Flags with less than twenty dollars in my pocket (even the drinks costs more than that) when most of my classmates had fifty dollars or more to spend. I learned how to navigate uncomfortable conversations about money and say, "Nah, I don't see anything I want," while secretly starving or hoping my friends would offer me some of theirs.

I wish I had known that not having souvenir and snack money had nothing to do with my worth as a person. I later learned that I have control over how I see and feel about myself. We will talk about that too as you work through this book.

When I lived in California, during lunchtime, my classmates each had different types of food inside their lunch box. And I had never been judged for the meals that my family would pack for me to eat. But in Illinois, I was suddenly being made fun of because of the fried chicken my mom packed for me at my new school.

One of my favorite things to eat was and is my dad's fried chicken. And now that same meal had me wanting to crawl under the lunch table because of some of the stupid things my classmates would say about Black people and fried chicken. I didn't know there was some lunch etiquette that I should have been aware of, until my white classmates pointed out the differences between my food and theirs. And not in a way that made me feel good about myself, but that left me sometimes hating my new life and my new friends.

I went from loving my life, because I felt such a strong sense of belonging, to feeling alienated and isolated. The other kids in Illinois had never had exposure to families that didn't look like them, and I had to bear the cost of their ignorance. It was a burden I learned to carry as a child, and it would affect me for the rest of my life.

I dealt with so many new emotions that boiled down to socioeconomic factors and being a Black girl in a small, white town. Of course, at that age, I just thought life was so unfair to Black girls. And maybe you think it's still unfair! Unfortunately, as my white friends lived out their teenage years wearing rose-colored glasses, I kept feeling the unfairness all the way through. I left high school, and by then—I didn't realize how much damage had been done.

Sigh

When I entered junior high school, it seemed like the innocence of my classmates shifted.

I used to think they didn't mean any harm by some of their statements, but now it started to feel like they were doubling down on their racism. I started to realize how taxing some of my relationships with my white friends were, but I didn't have the language to articulate what I was feeling or experiencing. To make matters worse, I was my white friends' only Black friend, and they looked at me like the keeper of all the Blackness.

There were days we would be sitting in the lunchroom and one of my white friends would say, "Minda, rap that one rap song, by Dr. Dre, we're sure you know the words." Or this expectation at recess to dance on command, because there is this assumption that all Black people must know how to dance. Anything they saw Black people doing that they felt was "cool" in a magazine or on television, they automatically expected I knew all about it because I was Black.

Maybe you have been your white friend's only Black or brown friend and you know how exhausting some of these relationships can be. Half the time, I didn't even know what they were referring to, because we didn't have cable and I wasn't allowed to listen to music that wasn't "church music" unless I was at a white friend's house and got to hear it there.

I was feeling left out inside and outside of my house. I felt pressure to be what my white friends felt Black people should be from their limited exposure to MTV and BET. And I was grappling with who I wanted to be as a Black girl, yet my environment made it hard to figure out how to balance the two. Meaning, I was trying to learn about myself and what it meant for me to be a Black girl, and wasn't obligated to be the Black girl from their music videos and teen magazines. But in school you sometimes feel you have to be who people want you to be so they will like you.

You might be thinking, why did I remain friends with these people? Or maybe you find yourself asking the same question to yourself regarding some of your friends. To be honest, I thought I didn't have any choice. I thought if I was going to live in a predominantly white town, then I needed to find some friends that would make being there a little more bearable, and over time I did find those friends. But knowing what I know now, and how it affected me, I should have created better boundaries, because I owed that to myself.

I hope you will consider letting your friends know what good looks like to you, especially when relationships don't make you feel like a healthy friendship should.

Here's one story about a time I wish I had set clear boundaries with my white friends.

In eighth grade, we could leave school at lunchtime and go off campus with our parent or guardian's permission. You had just enough time to walk about ten minutes up the street, where there were two gas stations and a popular pizza place. And just enough time to walk back. If you were not back to school in time, you would lose your off-campus privilege.

My mom and I had recently gotten the same new hairstyle, and we were feeling ourselves. It was a popular hairstyle you would see in all of the Black magazines. The only issue was that you had to use this spray that kept your hair looking kind of greasy and wet. But it was the style to have if you were Black in the early '90s.

At any rate, that Monday, I went to school with my new hairstyle. At lunch, I left campus with my friends to walk to get a slice of pizza. And as we walked up the street, we passed the high school. You would sometimes see the older kids on their lunch break too. Many of my girlfriends liked this because they got to see older boys they thought were cute.

As we walked past a group of white boys, one of them hollered out, "Hey Eazy-E." Now, I realize I am much older than you, and you probably have no idea who Eazy-E is: Eazy-E was a West Coast rapper. He rocked a similar hairstyle in the '80s, but when he had it, it was called a Jheri curl.

I had no idea who the boy was talking to. And at first, it was just one of the boys. Then they started chanting it together like they were part of a boy band: "Eazy-E! Eazy-E! Eazy-E!" Suddenly, I realized they were talking to *me*. Worse, all my friends laughed and called me a greaseball. "Don't touch Minda's hair, you'll need a towel afterwards," they joked—and that wasn't even the worst thing they said.

Let's just say that I chose not to go off campus for a while after that day. And I begged my mom to let me grow the wavy chemical out of my hair—I no longer wanted to be called a greaseball.

That was the moment I started to hate my hair. I wished I had hair like my white friends. And if I am being honest with you, thinking about that story still hurts. Because from that moment forward, I was acutely aware of any hairstyle I chose. I only chose hairstyles I thought the white kids wouldn't make fun of me for having.

Remember when I said I was trying to balance the two, figuring out who I wanted to be and who others wanted me to be? I loved that hairstyle and it was a popular hairstyle in the Black culture—and when I got it, the white kids made me the laughingstock of campus because they didn't understand my hair texture. Being Black seemed to become harder and harder by the day.

During this time in my life, I was feeling othered at every turn. And when you go through your tween and teenage years being made fun of by people who are supposed to be your friends, you unfortunately learn to start telling yourself that these white kids and their caregivers don't mean any harm. You slowly start to believe that maybe you don't belong, like you once thought you did. I learned to settle into subtle forms of racism and disrespect at a young age. And it was all of those experiences that caused me to shrink and slowly misplace my voice.

When I was growing up, there were days I secretly wished I could ask a genie in a bottle to grant me whiteness so I could belong. I now know I would never, ever want that wish to come true.

I love my skin way too much to be anybody else; I love *myself* way too much to be anybody else. Growing up in this environment was a tough time for me; I ain't gonna lie to you. But the good news is that I learned to love all parts of me, and I hope you continue to enjoy all the elements that make you, You! Because there is nothing wrong with you—but there are many things wrong with the status quo. (And if you have never heard of the word status quo, in the most simplest terms, it means the way folks have always done things. Doesn't mean we should do it this way, but it tends to be the norm.)

Rolling with the Homies

Just when I thought I might not be able to take it anymore, I met the Wilson girls, Stacie and Kendra.

They would only be in my life for two years before they moved away, but those two years made all the difference. I wasn't the only one anymore. Yo, it makes a difference when you're not the only Black girl rocking her Black girl braids. When the beads at the end seemed foreign to our other classmates, Stacie, Kendra, and I gave zero cares and click-clacked like nobody's business, giving them all the energy of a young Venus and Serena Williams. Those were some good times!

The Wilson girls and I also went to the same church. Before my dad started his church, we attended one of the only Black Baptist churches in town. And church was one of the only places I got to see the other Black people who lived in our new town. Since I had become friends with Stacie and Kendra from school, it was nice to also see familiar faces at church.

I got baptized when I was twelve, and that special moment in my life happened with my two new friends Stacie and Kendra by my side. All three of us got dunked under the water in the name of the Father, the Son, and the Holy Spirit. I had become way too familiar with alienation and isolation in Illinois, but when I met the Wilson girls I remembered what it felt like to belong again. And I felt like a million bucks!

One thing is certain: I have always loved having strong friendships with other Black and brown girls. We always got each other. That's why I included an entire chapter on friendship in this book. When you're feeling the isolation, it will be those friendships that help keep you grounded. By no means am I suggesting you won't have close friendships with girls and women who don't identify the way you do, but there is a special bond with other girls and women of color.

With Stacie and Kendra by my side, I learned there is power in numbers. For two years, I was reminded of the beauty of being Black. I had friends who looked like me to share experiences that didn't center on trying to fit in with the white kids. Sometimes I wonder how much I would have shrunk if I had never met Stacie and Kendra. Our friendship helped me love myself in ways I didn't realize I needed. I look forward to sharing more with you about my friendships and about the importance of having healthy relationships with your friends in the chapter called "What About Your Friends."

Why Wait

When I wrote my first book, *The Memo: What Women of Color Need to Know to Secure a Seat at the Table*, I thought about all the lessons I wish I had learned before I entered the workforce.

I quickly realized that I needed some of these life lessons way before entering corporate America. Soft skills like understanding your worth, finding your voice, and learning how to navigate systems that produce bias—Black and brown girls need that information, right now! (And if you're wondering what soft skills are: those tend to be things like communication skills, active listening, and things like time management. But in my opinion, there is nothing soft about those skills, we all need them.)

When I was traveling for my first book tour, I looked into the crowds of like minds and faces, and saw that some women would bring their daughters and nieces to my book talks. They'd whisper to me, "Gotta teach 'em young." I met fathers who purchased the book for their infant daughters, so they'd have a manual when they reached our age.

It struck me that we should start having these conversations at a much earlier age. I saw myself in their eyes. How much more hopeful would my life have been, back when I was struggling with being the only Black girl in my classroom in Illinois, if I'd had a big sister to guide me? If I'd had someone to remind me that everything I need is already inside of me?

What if I had the language as a young Black girl to help me articulate my place in this world, even when others questioned it? I wish I had known I could use my voice as a teen and that I didn't have to wait until I was an adult. If I had been encouraged to do so—I would have been a force to be reckoned with. Our minds are continually challenging the status quo, and for better or worse, this world shapes who we become.

I need you to know that you don't have to sweep your feelings under the rug to appease any group of people. You are the next generation to set this world ablaze, and we shouldn't wait to address the issues you face. It might be too late then! I need you to have the tools to show up in this world and be your brilliant self today! Because as our mutual friend Beyoncé said, "Brown skin girl . . . I'd never trade you for anybody else." And I don't want you ever to feel like you need to be anybody else. I need you to know that your feelings matter, and the world needs to know that too.

Oh, and trust me—Future You will thank you for doing the work now, so you can rock it out later.

Real Talk

It's no secret that I'm pretty excited to go on this journey with you.

I am the oldest of three kids and the only girl. I don't think my brothers appreciated all the advice I smothered them with. But, just like any older sister, I gave it to them anyway!

You Are More Than Magic will discuss many topics that I think will serve you well as you grow up, but most importantly, I want you to have the tools you need to enter college, join the workforce, or build your own table—meaning start your own company. The world is all yours!

There are kids just like you building companies and working to make the world a better place. There are young girls like Mikaila Ulmer, Naomi Wadler, Mari Copeny, and Marley Dias, who use their voices in ways I would never have imagined at your age. Let me tell you a little bit about these young girls that look just like you.

Mikaila Ulmer is a teen entrepreneur who started her lemonade business in Austin, Texas. You can now find her lemonade in stores like Whole Foods.

Naomi Wadler is using her teenage voice as an advocate against gun violence here in the United States, and she highlights how gun violence affects Black girls and women.

Mari Copeny, who is also known as Little Miss Flint, wrote a letter to then president Barack Obama, drawing his attention to the Flint Water Crisis in her hometown when she was just eight years old.

And last but not least, Marley Dias. When Marley was in elementary school she launched a book drive to donate one thousand books to Black girls at other schools. She wanted them to read books where Black girls were the main characters.

You have a voice just like these girls. You just have to decide how you want to use it. This world has space for you, you just have to decide how much space you want to take up!

What to Expect

I mentioned some of the hard times I had growing up Black, but that isn't the only thing this book is about.

We will discuss how to have tough conversations with adults, because part of using our voice requires us to be good communicators. Being a good communicator will also require you to have courage to discuss certain topics that might be taboo in some Black and brown households, or with your friends.

And, if you ever feel like you are being discriminated against, we will discuss how to advocate for yourself.

We'll discuss how to handle rejection or hear "no" in response to things you think you really wanted. I also have some advice about having a healthy mindset, because having a healthy way of thinking about yourself will be critical to your success as you get older. And I had a blast writing to you about lessons I learned on my first job at the Dairy Queen making Blizzards and writing very messy "Happy Birthday" messages on ice cream cakes.

As you make your way through the book, you won't just receive advice from me. I also conducted a series of roundtable discussions with young girls that look just like you. I asked them the same questions that I ask you in this book, and I included some of their thoughts and responses.

They were brutally honest with me about their experiences being Black and brown girls in junior high, high school, and college today. I learned so much from our conversations, and you will find that you are not alone in your experiences. One of the college girls that I interviewed, who lives in Indiana, told me that she just wants to feel "seen." She told me she is "tired" of being an afterthought to her white classmates. Listening to her speak reminded me of my own experiences.

My hope is that Black and brown girls won't be the only readers of this book, but that white kids who want to be better advocates and friends to their Black and brown friends, so they can feel "seen," will also read it. And I pray that white adults will pick up this book. It's important for white caregivers and teachers to read this book, because let's be honest, some of their problematic behaviors (intentional or unintentional) are harming Black and brown kids. And their actions are serving as a "role model" for their children—who will more than likely replicate the harm.

In order for Black and brown girls to walk in this world without feeling discriminated against and alienated in their classrooms or in the boardroom, we need all hands on deck to change the way the world works for all of us.

One Last Thing

I want you to know there was a time that I dealt with some of the same things you're experiencing or might experience one day. What type of big sister would I be if I didn't tell you everything I know?

I don't mind being vulnerable with you about some of my past experiences, so I hope you will trust me along this journey. You might feel alone now or unsure of where to place your new experiences—but you no longer have to wonder what next steps to take, because my goal by the end of this book is to equip you with all of the answers to those questions (or at least most of them). You never have to go through some of this stuff as the "only one" in your head—ever again.

I wrote this book so we can talk about these inequalities and experiences out loud. You are more than just some cute little saying like Black Girl Magic—you are so much more, and I hope you are already starting to realize that.

Oh, and before I forget. I wanted to tell you how to get the most out of reading or listening to *You Are More Than Magic*. As you might have already noticed, I've included "Quick Q's" to help you pause and marinate on some of the experiences I've shared with you and to help you reflect on your own. Also, at the end of each chapter is a section called "Show Me What You're Workin' With." This is a list of questions to help you navigate difficult situations you might be experiencing now or in the future.

And as you can see, I have already started opening up to you, so I hope you will open up to yourself when you get to this section and don't skip over it. Asking yourself the tough questions is part of standing in your brilliance. What you can confront, you can conquer! And you can conquer it all.

This book was written in a style that makes you feel like we are hanging out on a Friday night, chatting it up over some of our favorite snacks, while digging into life as we know it. And, because I got your back, there are resources at the end of this book for the adults in your life to help them be your best advocates and champions. So, without further ado—I will see you over in Chapter Two so we can get this slumber party started.

CHAPTER 2

More Than Magic

I have to tell you something about myself: I was considered one of those kids that were "old for their age." Or you might have heard some adults say, "They were here in another lifetime." I was that kid!

I was the kid having full-on conversations with adults at three years old. I grew up around a lot of adults, and for several years of my life, I was the only grandchild. Plus, like I said before, my mother is one of five girls. There was always someone talking to me.

When I was around eight years old, we lived in an apartment complex with five units. At one end of the building lived one of my aunts whom I affectionately call Aunt T. At the other end of the complex lived my parents' good friends from the Bahamas, the Joneses. We lived in the middle, and our home was like the nucleus of our little community.

Aunt T and I were thick as thieves. I would walk down the sidewalk to her house, hang out for hours, talk, eat sunflower seeds, and laugh. It's one of those childhood memories that I always look back on and smile.

Aunt T and I had a wonderful, honest relationship. I loved going to spend time with her. The only problem was that she smoked cigarettes. And I would leave her house smelling like a cigarette factory.

Now, she wasn't the only one with a vice. As mature as I thought I was, I was still sucking my thumb. I remember one day while we were hanging out, I said to her, "I wish you would stop smoking." She, in turn, said, "I wish you would stop sucking your thumb."

I was shocked, probably just as shocked as Aunt T was to hear me say what I said. I had to make a serious decision: Was my thumb worth it? I sat with our dialogue in my head for days. And to be honest, Aunt T liked smoking, and I liked sucking my thumb. What were two girls to do?

I told Aunt T that I love her, but it's hard to sit near her for long periods while she smokes. At that age, I knew absolutely nothing about self-advocacy, but I knew the smoke bothered me enough to tell her, for her health and mine. I had other relatives that smoked, but I felt like I could tell my aunt, and she would listen to me because she valued what I had to say, even at that age.

Initially, I had not factored in what her response might be to what I said to her. I thought we would just be talking about her not smoking anymore—now the discussion included what she would like to see me stop doing. I told Aunt T that I needed more time to think about what I was willing to give up to see one of my favorite people stop smoking.

Within a week, I came up with my grand plan! I presented this plan to her as if I were in a boardroom. I proposed that if she gave up smoking, I would stop sucking my thumb. Now, I don't remember everything that happened afterward, but Aunt T weaned herself off cigarettes and I stopped sucking my thumb. It was a win-win for both parties. And we still joke about that conversation when we see each other.

Looking back on my childhood and teenage years, I guess you could say I've been doing some form of self-advocacy all my life. You probably have too. Those times you've asked to stay up just a little later—that counts! Or when you begged to go to a friend's house, but you had homework to do—that counts too. Oh, and instead of having chicken noodle soup for dinner, you pleaded for pizza. All of these experiences required self-advocacy in some way, shape, or form. And guess what? You've been standing up for yourself at times you probably didn't even realize it.

Tell Me More

You still might be wondering, what is self-advocacy? I'm glad you asked.

According to Dictionary.com, self-advocacy is "the act or condition of representing oneself." There are times in each of our lives when we have to represent, or stand up for, ourselves.

Standing up for yourself won't ever stop. It's a muscle I still push myself to flex to this very day. Some of us may have an easy time vocalizing our thoughts, and some of us might start sweating at just the thought of it. Self-advocacy is a tool that I want you to have in your life's toolkit, because once you understand who you are and what you're worth, you won't let anyone steal your magic or your joy.

Self-advocacy is especially essential for girls like us—Black and brown girls. Sometimes society will tell us our opinions don't matter, or due to our various shades of melanin, we should be happy with the opportunities we've received. But Harriet Tubman didn't spend over ten years of her life helping more than three hundred enslaved people escape to freedom so that you and I could question ourselves. We have to learn to stand in our truth when courage calls us to the microphone.

When you use your voice, it often sparks something in others and creates a chain reaction. Maybe your voice will inspire the next Black or brown girl to own her voice as well. We all have a voice, and you get to decide how and when to use yours!

If you had asked me as a teenager what self-advocacy was, I would have probably thought it had something to do with "talking back" or "getting smart" with adults. When I was younger, it seemed like every time I had a difference of opinion with my dad, he would tell me to "stop getting smart with him." To be fair, I am sure there were times I might have been sassy, but other times, I legitimately just wanted to voice my concerns about something I was experiencing in that moment.

I'm sure you have heard it before—when a parent or adult

tells you something, and you disagree or have an alternate opinion, they might decide you're being disrespectful. Perhaps if more adults understood how important self-advocacy is for their Black and brown girls, they would never silence their kids' voices, and young Black and brown girls could leverage the power they have to articulate their values, dreams, and goals.

If you learn to advocate for yourself now, it will be so much easier to advocate for yourself when the stakes are higher later on. Sometimes you'll be the only person who is able to advocate on your own behalf, and I don't want you waiting on someone else to advocate for you, when I know you have a voice ready to speak its truth. If you can find your voice now, you'll be able to use it in school to speak up about an unfair grade, and you'll be able to use it in your career to negotiate your salary or take a sick day when you need it.

Your future self will thank you for having a skill that will serve you in school, at home, and at work.

In this chapter, as you can probably already tell, we are going to talk about how you can best advocate for yourself and why self-advocacy will be a necessary skill set for the rest of your life. Showing up for ourselves and being clear about the things that matter most to us is an act of self-love. We might not be able to control the outcome of every situation, but I guarantee you will never regret learning to speak your truth.

I will share with you how I found my voice even when I wasn't convinced I had one. And we will discuss how to identify situations that might require self-advocacy at school, with family members, or with your friends, and what steps you can take to make sure you are saying what you mean, without saying it mean.

What Does It Look Like?

I can tell you about a few examples of times that I had to advocate for myself when I was a teenager. Maybe they'll remind you of your own experience.

When I was sixteen years old, my parents had a house rule that all the kids had to be home before ten p.m. My parents were very firm about ten p.m. being my curfew. When I turned seventeen years old, most of my friends were turning eighteen years old, and they could stay out until midnight. I hated always being the one that had to go home at ten and then hear about all that fun that happened between ten and midnight that did not include me.

After feeling left out more times than I can count, I asked my parents if they would consider extending my curfew until midnight if I promised to keep them in the loop about where I was hanging out. At first, I received a no, but over time my parents thought about it and extended my curfew to midnight. In this case, advocating for myself was a good thing—I no longer missed out on the extended fun.

Another example of self-advocacy from around the same time happened on the night of my junior prom. Before the dance, my date took me to a restaurant for dinner. When we got to the restaurant, we ended up waiting at our table for over an hour before our food came out. When the food finally arrived at the table, it was cold.

Me and my date Johnny were so annoyed. We had both saved up money to enjoy this fancy restaurant. At first, we were just going to eat the meal, pay for it, and move on with our lives. But something inside of me felt like one of us needed to let the waitress know that our food was cold and ask if we could have a new meal or a discount on the food—so I did.

She said that it would take another hour before we could get another plate. We didn't have another hour available to wait or we would be late to the dance. So, I made a bold move and told her that we would be leaving and would not be paying for cold food, that, in my opinion, was not edible. She did not like that response and brought her manager over to the table, but in the end, my self-advocacy won out.

When all was said and done, we didn't have to pay and ended up getting KFC to eat on the hour-long ride back to the dance. In this case, it wasn't the most comfortable experience because I could tell the adults we were interacting with felt like we were just kids and didn't have any right to complain. But what I learned that day is that we always have agency if the situation matters to us!

I was so nervous in that restaurant! But I didn't want us to use our hard-earned money on food and service that was subpar. If it had been up to our waitress and her manager, they probably would have charged us. But there was no way we were going to pay seventy-five dollars for cold food. I worked too hard at my minimum-wage job to spend my money like that. On the ride to the dance, Johnny hyped me up because he had never seen me take control and advocate in that way. We both were surprised!

Back then, I didn't know that asking to stay out later or not paying for our cold food was self-advocacy. I just felt like both situations were unfair, and I needed to address them. I found the parts I had control over: I could tell my parents what I wanted my curfew to be; I could tell the waitress the cold food was not okay; I could use my voice. And every time I advocated for myself after that, it got a little easier each time.

You might find that you tend to do more advocating at home and others might find that most of their advocating happens on the field or in the classroom. There probably won't be an area of your life that won't require you to advocate for yourself in some capacity. And self-advocacy won't always be done in person. Sometimes it might be on the phone or via email or text. There are many ways to advocate for yourself and hopefully get closer to an outcome you are pleased with.

Again, even if the situation doesn't turn in your favor after you've said what you need, I hope you will never regret using your voice!

Courage

After hearing or reading those two examples I gave, you might be thinking to yourself, there is no way I could do that. There was a time in my life that I didn't think I could do that either, but with practice, I find that advocating for myself isn't as scary as it sounds.

Have you heard of the saying *practice makes perfect*? Well, if you need help figuring out what you want to communicate or advocate for, you can always write yourself a script and practice saying it in the mirror, recording yourself and playing it back, or practicing with someone you trust. I think that might be a good place for you to start if you aren't used to asking for what you want.

Let *me* start by asking you some questions. The last time you had to stand up for yourself, how did it make you feel? Was it hard? Would you do it again if you had to? I'm not sure how you answered each question, but I can imagine that sometimes you might have felt scared or not as brave as you thought you could be. Trust me, you are not alone. It takes a lot of courage to advocate for yourself. The late great Dr. Maya Angelou said:

"Courage is the most important of all the virtues. Because without courage, you cannot practice any other virtue consistently. You can be kind for a while; you can be generous for a while; you can be just for a while, or merciful for a while, even loving for a while. But it is only with courage that you can be persistently and insistently kind and generous and fair."

Self-advocacy might sound like a fancy term to throw around, yet it's so much more than that! Advocating for yourself is revolutionary, because not everyone is courageous enough to activate their own voice to center themself. When we don't advocate for ourselves when the situation calls for it, we are conditioning the silence of our voices. And if Black and brown girls aren't advocating for ourselves, how will other people know what we like and what doesn't fly with us?

We need your voice because your opinions and experiences matter. I want the people in your life, at home, at school, and out in the world to know when they have done right by you and when they have fallen short. Again, self-advocacy requires some courage, and I can't wait to see you lean into it!

Advocacy in Action

Now that you understand what self-advocacy is, let's look at how you might activate it in your life.

First, let's take a look at how self-advocacy could work at school. You might receive a grade that you feel isn't reflective of your hard work in your English class, and you have this feeling in the pit of your stomach that you need to talk to your teacher about it. Now, in this case, there are many ways you might go about advocating for yourself:

You might decide that you don't want to do anything about it, because you have told yourself that nothing is going to change, so why bother. But if you don't "bother," then you're going to drive yourself crazy about this final grade.

You might talk to your parent or guardian about the situation and ask them to help you figure out what to do about your grade. This is one form of self-advocacy.

You could choose to take your self-advocacy all the way to the top by emailing your teacher and asking to schedule a time to discuss your grade.

The thing you should keep in mind about self-advocacy is that you might not get the outcome you want. The part of the equation that *you* can always solve is what you choose to do and how you handle it. I wish I could give you another equation that makes the person or people on the receiving end of your self-advocacy tell you what you need to hear for a positive outcome. But the truth is, we can't control anything beyond ourselves.

Previously, I told you about two situations where I had to advocate for myself that eventually played out in my favor. But, what I haven't told you about yet are all the times my self-advocacy didn't end with a win. Not everything will always go our way, but I have never been mad that I showed up for myself.

One summer, I was hired for a job where I was expected to work every Saturday. But every summer before I took that position, I loved playing in a basketball tournament that took up one whole weekend every June. Now I had a conflict: I was required to work every Saturday, but I also loved playing in that tournament. I would have to ask my manager if I could have that Saturday off.

I must admit, I was nervous about asking for the day off because I didn't know how my manager would respond. For a brief moment, I thought maybe I just wouldn't play that year because I didn't want to ask for the time off. Two things ran through my mind: 1) They are going to fire me if I ask for time off, and 2) Maybe I can quit and find a new job.

I talked it over with my parents. They encouraged me to speak with my manager and ask for the time off in advance and not to wait until the last minute. Remember a few pages ago, when I said self-advocacy takes courage? That's the same courage I needed to use to ask for the time off.

I explained the situation to my manager and asked whether she would consider letting me swap out one of my Saturdays for a day during the week. With no hesitation, and even though I offered to make up the time for the Saturday I needed off, she said no.

The thing that hurt the most about her saying no to me was that this would be the last year I could play in this tournament before I went off to college. I tried my best to appeal to her softer side, but nothing changed her answer. Yet, even though I didn't hear the answer I wanted (and despite being upset), I was still glad I asked her about the time off and presented my case. Just like I had a choice to ask or not, she had a choice to let me have the time off or not.

Self-advocacy isn't about getting the answer you want, it's about letting people know what you need by using your voice.

No matter what answer you receive, I hope you will always know that it was worth it!

Oh, and I ended up working that Saturday and did not play in the tournament. I knew that I had made a commitment to work on Saturdays and made the decision to stick to my commitment.

I also want you to understand that everything doesn't have to be a fight. Please don't confuse self-advocacy with being argumentative. After my manager said no to that Saturday off, I could have decided to keep going back and forth with her and make it an issue, but that was not the goal. The goal was to express that I would like time off, explain why I was asking for the time off, and offer up an alternative day that I could work to make up the hours. After I had done that, I had to make the choice to let it go.

Here is what I would like you to keep in mind regardless of what happens after you advocate for yourself. Ask yourself these questions:

- **Am I being honest about what I am advocating for?**
- **Even if my advocacy doesn't result in moving my needs forward, how can I still view this as a win because I spoke my truth?**

Please make sure that you are advocating for something that matters to you. There might be times that one of your friends pressures you to advocate for something that you don't really want. So when you face situations like that, I would like for you to ask yourself one more question:

- Do I really want what I am advocating for or do I feel pressured to advocate for it by someone else?

By asking yourself these questions, you can make sure that you are truly advocating for yourself for the right reasons. And if at any time you aren't sure if you're advocating for the right reasons, go back to the earlier part of this chapter and revisit the definition I gave you for self-advocacy and make sure that your *actions* are aligned with your *values*.

There have been so many times in my life that I let something slide even though I knew I should have shown up for myself. Sometimes, we imagine the worst outcome, and that keeps us from speaking our truth, being honest about how we feel, and investigating possible solutions. There's no harm in having a thoughtful conversation with someone who can help you. It's time we start trying to imagine the best outcome instead.

We have to hold on to everything that makes us more than magic. When we let others dictate our narratives—our life stories—or our futures, we allow others to chip away at us, until we only have little pieces of ourselves left.

And little sis, you need your entire voice, not little pieces of it!

An Act of Love

I want you to know that self-advocacy is tied to self-esteem. It's not about how others see us, but how we see ourselves.

We have to learn how to put some respect on our own names.

For example, you're at a party that all the cool kids are at (can you see me rolling my eyes as I write this?), and your curfew is eleven p.m. and not a minute later. While having a good time at the party, you see the person you've been crushing on and walk toward them to say hi. Next thing you know, it's 10:30 p.m., and your conversation is going way too well to end it in the next fifteen minutes. You casually mention that you have to leave soon, and they try to convince you to stay longer, and that breaking curfew is worth it.

Now, let's be honest: Even if you stayed longer and missed curfew, you wouldn't fully enjoy yourself because you'd be thinking about the aftermath when you get home and face your parent or guardian. Additionally, your crush shouldn't encourage you to get grounded before they even get a chance to take you on the first date.

I know what you're thinking: Minda, how is this self-advocacy? Watch and see. I'm guessing you're the type of person who likes to play by the rules, and you want to make it home on time, but you're torn! There are a couple of ways to advocate for yourself in this situation: 1) You message your family and ask if you can stay out a little longer, or 2) You tell your crush that if they want to see you again, you have to head home. And that means you have to go now. And exchange numbers and plan to hang out soon. The end and happily ever after!

You are in a tough spot, and you have the choice to take your power back. Why? Because you value your family rules, your time, and your worth. And, if someone is into you, they won't encourage you to break the rules.

Self-advocacy isn't easy, but remember when I told you it was a form of self-love? If we learn to love ourselves, then we ain't got time for anyone to mistreat us.

It Can Change Your Life—If You Let It

Self-advocacy doesn't only mean standing up for yourself; it means advancing yourself and growing too.

Have I told you about the time I wanted to learn how to ride horses? I was around fourteen or fifteen years old and vehemently wanted to learn the art of horseback riding, but my family couldn't afford lessons. But I wasn't about to let lack of money stop me.

So what did I do? I did my research and compiled a list of all the closest horse stables. Then I called all of them and asked if I could speak to the owner. I explained that I did not have the financial resources to pay for lessons, but I wanted to propose an exchange: I could help keep the stables clean, and in return, the stable owner would teach me for free.

I received a lot of no's, but I did get a yes from a modest barn owned by two sisters. And that is how your girl learned how to ride horses.

The story doesn't end there. These generous sisters lived a couple of towns over, and I needed transportation to the barn. So I had to advocate for myself again and ask my parents to drive me to the lessons and pick me up. I think they were surprised by my initiative and self-advocacy, but they supported me in the ways I needed them to.

When I started talking to the stable owners and to my parents, I didn't know what the outcome would be, but I was determined, and I leaned into the part of the equation that I had control over—me. I often think about how I almost missed out on learning how to ride a horse. I'm so grateful that, instead of missing out, I learned to activate my voice.

You Can Do It

Author and former late-night TV host Craig Ferguson has helped me in ways he doesn't know. He suggests that we ask ourselves three questions:

- **Does this need to be said?**
- **Does this need to be said by me?**
- **Does this need to be said right now?**

This is one framework I use when I am trying to decide *when* to advocate for myself. Timing is key. Sometimes, we need to advocate for ourselves in the moment, but sometimes we might need to wait until we've gathered a little more information or sought out some advice from a friend or family member.

Let's think about the example of the bad grade you didn't agree with. It's a grade for the whole semester, so this is a big deal. Before talking to your teacher, you can ask yourself, "Does this need to be said?" In other words, do you need to advocate for yourself in this situation? Well, you believe your hard work deserves a higher grade. Plus, it's bothering you so much that the only way you'll be able to let it go is by speaking up.

Yes, you decide: It needs to be said.

On to the second question: "Does this need to be said by me?" Your parent or guardian could reach out and talk to your teacher, but they probably wouldn't be the best people to articulate your needs to a professor they've never met. Now, in a different situation, perhaps you might need an adult to help you advocate, and that's okay too. But in this one, the answer to the second question is yes, it needs to be said by me.

Lastly, "Does this need to be said right now?" In this case, you might want to take a minute to make sure you're presenting the best possible case. Do you have evidence of how your work improved over the course of the semester? Can you show that you participated in class every day, or talk to a friend about how your work compared on a test? Could you offer to do extra credit?

It's time-sensitive—you need to have the conversation soon so that your teacher can (possibly) make the change before they turn in final grades. But it makes sense to gather all the information you need before having the conversation. That way, you can be your best advocate.

This framework helps me decide when I need to raise my voice and when I need to chill. I hope you will leverage these questions when you're trying to figure out whether your advocacy is urgent or you have a little more time to make a decision about your next steps.

You Have Access Already

Self-advocacy is a tool we all have access to, you just have to decide if you want to use it.

One of my favorite poets, Audre Lorde, said, "Beware of feeling like you're not good enough to deserve it." You always deserve for someone to hear you out. They won't always agree with you, but you deserve their respect, and that means having your voice heard. And the sooner you understand that, the easier self-advocacy will become.

Self-advocacy doesn't mean you have to do everything yourself. My parents always helped me make sure I was on the right path and thinking through my next steps. Yes, I was the one advocating, but I always had the support of my family, so I didn't feel like I was alone when I asked for what I needed. And hopefully, you have some people in your life that you can lean on when you are nervous and need some additional support.

The next time you think about standing up for yourself, remember these five steps along the way:

Center your narrative around honesty and your need to be heard. Remind yourself that you aren't complaining and you aren't nagging. You're initiating a healthy dialogue and advocating for a solution that is based on your needs.

Check in with yourself. This is important. You have to ask yourself the tough questions, like, "Does this situation require me to step into my courage, or should I lay low?" Never base your advocacy around what others think is a big deal or not. Only you can make that call for YOU. We will talk more about this later in the book—so keep reading!

Just add courage. Self-advocacy requires us to lean into our courage and push aside our caution, because we will never be our best advocates when we operate from a place of fear.

Practice, practice, practice. If you need to, you can write out the words you want to say and practice how those words sound coming from you. Role-play various scenarios so that you feel more comfortable and prepared.

Ask for help if you need it. Sometimes we will have to go into the arena alone, but don't forget to tap into your community when you need it. Success is not a solo sport!

I hope you find that self-advocacy is a powerful tool at your disposal if you activate your voice. And just think about how much better this world will be with so many more Black and brown girls advocating for themselves. The end result will be that people get used to hearing our voices and seeing how powerful we are. I can't wait for you to share more of your voice and be part of the revolution!

Show Me What You're Workin' With

Now it's time to make self-advocacy real. I've given you some examples and ways to think about how self-advocacy can help you own any room you walk into—because the world is waiting for your voice. Nobody is going to advocate for you better than you can for yourself. Use this section to reflect and think about how to seize your next opportunity to let someone know that you are more than magic.

1) Where do you find yourself most in need of self-advocacy (at home, at school, at work, with friends)? Why?

2) What is one way that you will commit to advocating for yourself in the next thirty days?

3) How do you think self-advocacy can help you as you dream bigger dreams and reach your goals?

4) If, for some reason, a self-advocacy conversation doesn't go the way you planned, what's one word that you will reflect on to remind yourself that you did what was best for you?

5) Who are the people in your life that you can call on when you need to ask for help?

CHAPTER 3

Don't Stop, Get It

As you have probably learned by now, there will be times in your life where things go absolutely the way you hoped they would, and there will be times when you have to hit the reset button and try again next time.

Maybe there have been times when you asked your mom if you could stay overnight at your best friend's house and without hesitation, she said YES. And because she said yes, you had the time of your life staying up all night long, eating junk food, and gushing over your latest crush! But I'm sure you also remember those moments when she said no, and you felt like you would probably be missing out on a night of fun and the world was about to end. When you're a teenager, those are two emotions you feel just about every day.

I have so many memories of big feelings from those years that still bring a smile to my face. For example, I loved it when my dad would walk through the door and yell out, "Who wants to go for a ride?" My family of five would run from their various parts of our home, and we would all pile into the car. Everybody loved those car rides.

It was even more fun when I had my learner's permit, so I was the one who got to drive us around town. What I loved most about those car rides was that no matter how old I got, and no matter how busy my brothers were with their respective sports, we always made time to be together. In the car, we let ourselves slow down and have conversations about what was going on in our lives, and we could all weigh in.

On those car rides, my parents would always remind me and my brothers that sometimes the world can be cruel to Black and brown kids, but to always remember that we were young kings and queens. They would remind us that just because someone called us a name or denied us access to something we wanted, their "no" didn't mean we weren't good enough!

My mom would always say, "As long as *you* know." What she meant—and what I'm telling you—is that other people don't know our ability to keep striving toward our dreams, but we do! I always appreciated those reminders because outside of that car, we really needed them. We needed them when we didn't make the team. We needed them when we had a hard time making friends. And we needed them when we encountered systems of oppression and racism.

I'm glad that my parents instilled a sense of self-worth inside me and my brothers at a young age, because it helped me continue to build my resilience as I got older. There were times in my youth when I wanted certain things like making the basketball team or the cheerleading team, only to be met with a "no" each time. It was those car rides that helped ease the pain of hearing "no." And let's be honest, as Black and brown girls, we might hear the word "no" more than some of our white friends.

In my town, a lot of the teachers and coaches were white. For my white friends, that meant the coaches identified with them because they reminded them of a younger version of themselves. Unfortunately, I didn't get the opportunity to be viewed the same way, and that experience is the same for Black and brown girls all over America. The ugly truth is that sometimes, we receive a "no" and we know it's not that we didn't earn a spot on the team or that our work on that essay wasn't good enough. We know the "no" was race-related.

Some of those moments might make us feel like we don't even want to get out of bed and get ready for school in the morning. But even though those experiences were terrible, I learned resilience. I knew that I could control *me*, and that realization helped me become a better version of myself today. And I hope some of your experiences will turn out to help build your resilience too.

In this chapter we are going to discuss what to do when you are told "no." Hearing "no" might make you feel like you weren't the chosen one, and that is a normal emotion to feel when we are disappointed with an outcome.

But guess what! Someone else saying "no" isn't the end of your story. You have a choice: You can reframe what might feel like failure. You can access your inner strength to help build your resilience and continue to see yourself as more than magic. In this chapter, I will provide you with a framework to help you push forward. You cannot give up on your dreams just because you get a "no," because your "yes" might be right around the corner.

I Got Some No's

Have you ever tried out for the school play or a sports team? Have you ever applied for a job you really wanted? Then you know: You'll always be nervous as you wait for the results, and sometimes, you'll get a disappointing answer.

I want to tell you about the time I tried out for my school's cheerleading team. I was so excited for this opportunity. My mom was a Pom-Pom in her high school days and she tried her best to transfer her skills over to me. She practiced the routines with me for a few days before the tryouts. On the day of tryouts, I gave it everything I had and left it all on the floor!

A few days later, I checked the little white paper outside of the locker room only to be met with disappointment. My name wasn't on the list. The coach decided to go with a squad of blonde and brunette white girls—not one Black or brown girl was chosen.

I was mad, I was disappointed, and I couldn't help but wonder if maybe, had I attended a more diverse school, I might've had the opportunity to be a cheerleader. Unfortunately, we'll never know for sure. What I do know is that I felt isolated, I felt confused, and I couldn't help but wonder why the coach would choose a team of all white girls, when there were some really good girls of color to choose from as well. After I saw that my name wasn't on the list, I ran home and cried.

Most of all, I remember feeling sad because I felt unseen. And I wish I could tell you that that was the last time I felt that way, but that would be a lie.

I want to pause and first talk to you about the concept of being chosen. When I wasn't picked for the cheerleading team, I went down a dangerous mental rabbit hole, telling myself that maybe I wasn't pretty enough or good enough—even though *I* saw myself as pretty and good enough.

Receiving a no or feeling like you have not been chosen for something is painful. Unfortunately, some of us might live in a community or a country that doesn't always value girls that look like me and you. There are false narratives that Black and brown girls are too loud, too sassy, or too . . . *something* that makes the dominant majority question or judge us differently than white girls.

Quick Q's: **Have you ever dealt with a situation like this?**

Choose Yourself

When I didn't get picked for the cheerleading squad, it hurt.

I cried about not being one of the "chosen." I will never

know if that coach was racist or whether he even realized that he had picked only white girls for the squad, but I couldn't allow his bias to dictate my worth. And even though I wasn't chosen for the team, I still was able to choose how I viewed my self-worth. That is something that you will always have control over.

When we put too much value on someone else's idea of our worth, we discount how we see ourselves. Just because someone doesn't choose us doesn't mean we aren't worthy of future yeses and better opportunities down the road.

If you stay going down that negative self-talk rabbit hole, you are actively choosing to adopt negative thoughts about yourself. And that type of thinking will only make matters worse and won't make you feel better in the long run. Also, once you're in that negative state of mind, you might lean into it even when you are met with the answer you want! You might find yourself questioning *why* they choose you, instead of celebrating your success (this is called imposter syndrome, and we'll talk more about it in Chapter Seven).

I want to remind you of another quote from Dr. Maya Angelou: "You may not control all the events that happen to you, but you can decide not to be reduced by them." I'd like you to always remember those words when you are treated unfairly or unkindly or when you don't receive equal treatment to white girls. You might not be able to control the decisions that your teachers, coaches, or caregivers make when it comes to you, but you will always have the choice to decide that you are still more than magic.

Resilience

Unfortunately, the word "no" will follow you out of your teenage years and into the rest of your life. From the job you don't get a call back from, to the college that doesn't admit you, to going through your first breakup, you will always have those "no" experiences, but it's the lessons you learn from them and the way you choose to grow through them that count.

When I didn't make the cheerleading squad, I had two choices: to become bitter, or to move forward. You will be faced with the same choices someday.

I began to use those no's to flex my resilience muscle. In my opinion, life is a series of adjustments to situations that don't always go our way. The adjustment might be uncomfortable, the change might even cause you pain, but you can withstand the shock, because you were built for so many more yeses. In other words, no's come but you don't have to constantly continue to play them on a loop. You can choose to be resilient and move forward.

When I started my company, The Memo LLC, I set out to help other women of color feel seen in the workplace. The feeling of wanting to be "seen" and "chosen" doesn't go away when you become an adult. I created The Memo LLC to serve as an advocate to help women of color see their worth in the workplace, so we can be promoted and get paid equally.

One of my company's core values is resilience. Being resilient isn't something that just happens to us overnight. Being resilient is a muscle that we have to learn to strengthen and flex every day of our lives. And the sooner you understand how to dust yourself off and try again, the more you'll thrive later on.

It took time for me to understand how to be resilient, but I made resilience part of my everyday life. In other words, resilience isn't a one-time event, it's a lifestyle. So even though I didn't make the cheerleading team, I didn't give up on myself. I still believed that I had a role to play somewhere and goals to achieve.

Try It Again, Even If You're Scared

Before we move on, let's discuss fear and insecurities a little bit more.

It's an important part of the resilience equation. After a disappointment, it's natural to feel worried about trying again. Resilience won't cure that fear, but it will help you push past it. There will always be something in life that scares you, especially if you are scared of hearing no again. But I hope you'll let your curiosity be bigger than your fears or insecurities.

When I was younger, I had so many insecurities around being one of the only Black girls at school and in our community. I was always wondering if I wasn't getting chosen for opportunities due to the color of my skin, and that question almost paralyzed me. No one should have to constantly ask herself whether she's being judged fairly, and no one should let that worry dictate what's possible for her.

So the next time you feel scared to try out for something

because you're worried about being rejected again, I want you to let your inner voice remind you that you are more than enough. And while you're reminding yourself of that, I also created five affirmations that I want you to use when you feel scared or insecure about going after something you really want. Because the part of the equation that you can solve is giving it your best shot!

- I belong, and I will continue to be aware of the places that I plant myself so I am positioned to grow. And if these people, places, and things don't contribute to my growth, I have the courage to move on.
- I honor my talents, ideas, and my ability to control my own actions.
- I have the ability to create my own narrative and I have the power to define my success.
- I release fear, anxiety, and insecurities. There is no room in my future for things that don't add value to my life.
- My racial identity belongs to me and no one can stop my progress because I control my destiny.

Now, I know what you might be thinking: "Really, Minda, affirmations?" But trust me. There will be days when you might not be able to get in touch with your best friend, or maybe your guardian or relatives are busy. But the tool that is always available to you is your positive inner and outer self-talk.

Many of these affirmations are based on the car rides I had

with my family. My parents would always remind me how resilient I am, and eventually, I started to believe them!

Before you decide that you're too cool for affirmations, please try them out. If they don't help, you can go back to whatever you were doing before, deal?

There will always be voices, both inside ourselves and from the world outside, that try to chip away at us and make us feel less than. Remember: You have a stronger inner voice that has the ability to speak to you with love, care, and courage! You were made to thrive, and you were built for greatness.

A Bump in the Road

I want to share another story with you. It happened the same year as the cheerleading tryout gone wrong.

I was a huge athlete back then. I ran track and played basketball. I loved sports, which is funny now because if you didn't know me back then, you would have no idea that I ever had an interest in sports. Running the 100-meter dash was my first love and playing basketball came in a close second. I participated in both sports starting in grade school, and I even played in summer leagues.

I never thought I was good enough to play professionally, but I was quick and knew how to handle the ball. So it was natural for me to try out for the team in junior high.

Once again, I gave it my best shot. I was a much better

basketball player than a cheerleader, so I just knew I would make the team. But when I looked at the paper outside of the locker room, I saw that I didn't make the starting team, which was called "the A team." If you didn't see your name on the starting team, that meant you could automatically play on the school's secondary team—"the B team." (Now that I think about it, sheesh, couldn't they have come up with a better name so B team players wouldn't feel bad?)

Once again, I felt many of the same emotions I had when I wasn't picked for the cheerleading squad. I was upset because I knew some of the girls that were picked for the A team and I knew I had more game than they did. I almost didn't want to play at all if I couldn't have what I really wanted. But this time, the coach had chosen one Black girl and one brown girl, and the remaining team members on the A team were white. This was a prime opportunity for me to use some of the tools we discussed earlier about self-talk and resilience.

Even though I was deeply disappointed, I decided to choose an empire state of mind instead of an enemy state of mind. Let me explain: An *empire state of mind* is reminding yourself you can make it anywhere and nothing anyone says or does can ruin your plans. An *enemy state of mind* is that negative inner voice we discussed earlier in this chapter; it will only hold you back. We cannot actively choose to be our own enemy—that is counterproductive.

I decided not to give up on my love of basketball just because things didn't turn out the way I had envisioned them. I thought,

I still like this game, so I'll do my best on the B team and see how I can make lemonade out of lemons.

On the B team, I was able to hone my skills, and I actually got to be a starting player. I asked myself: What if I did make the A team and I only sat on the bench and never got to play? Would it have been enough just to say that I made the team but never played? No, I would have hated every minute. I would have missed out on actually playing a game I loved, just to say I was on the A team.

Originally, I thought being on the B team was a massive failure, but as time went on, my mindset shifted. I was able to see my opportunity to learn and become a better player. And this mindset shift helped me build an even stronger resilience muscle. I chose to maintain my empire state of mind throughout my time on the B team.

Quick Q's: **Can you think of an experience that felt horrible at first, but ended up being better for you in the end?**

No Failures Here

Maybe your inner voice's default mode is negative, and it's constantly telling you you're a failure and a bunch of other nonsense. But I hope you'll fight extra hard to silence that voice.

You can use those affirmations I told you about—they'll help!

I don't believe that any of us are failures, but moments of disappointment happen, so we can learn from them and try again when we are ready.

Sometimes as girls we put so much pressure on ourselves to hit the bull's-eye the first time, and we don't leave any room for patience and growth. Don't forget to always be kind to yourself!

Vote for Me

I told you about two moments in my teenage years when I received a no that I wasn't expecting. A year later, I decided that I was ready to try my hand again at something new: I wanted to run for student council secretary.

Being part of student council would allow me to serve in a leadership role and represent the needs of the students. I had no formal experience. I just knew that I wanted to make my school better than I found it. Plus, there were currently no student leaders of color, so I definitely wanted to make sure our needs were articulated to leadership.

Running for student council was very different from trying out for the basketball team. I consider myself a baller, so trying out for the team was a no-brainer. But when it came to student council, I wasn't sure I was qualified.

The only leadership role I'd ever had was babysitting, if you count that (I do! Managing kids is great leadership experience).

Even though I wanted to join the student council, I kept thinking about what happened to me when I tried out for basketball and cheerleading. Those experiences haunted me, but I had to fight them off like a horror film heroine. I wouldn't let them get me!

Still, I almost let one of my fears stop me dead in my tracks, and that was my fear of public speaking. If I did end up becoming the secretary, I would have to take notes, or what they called "minutes," of what was discussed and then read them out loud during our meetings. I was okay with everything up till "read out loud." And to make matters worse, I would have to give a campaign speech to even run for the job!

I always loved the idea of public speaking but only in theory, not so much in practice. Yet, I was still willing to try my best just as I did with basketball and cheerleading. I remember having to work really hard to suppress that enemy state of mind and replace it with an empire state of mind.

I have a question for you: What will you do when your fears start to make you feel like you can't try again? I hope your curiosity about what's on the other side of your fear will push you forward—that is the part of the equation you have control over!

I had to lean into my curiosity and courage and push aside my fear. I couldn't very well read the minutes as the dopest and freshest secretary alive if 1) I never ran, and 2) I let my fear of the unknown get in my way. I reminded myself that I deserved this position just as much as anyone else in my grade.

So I leaned into my empire state of mind! Sometimes we can be our own worst enemy, but I wasn't going to let that enemy state of mind win. I decided to run.

Even today, I still keep my curiosity front and center, and so far, it has kept me from giving in to my fears. The late activist and singer Nina Simone said, "I'll tell you what freedom is to me; no fear, I mean really, no fear!" I hope you'll allow yourself to be free from fear too.

Quick Q's: **How will you lean into your curiosity and courage and push aside your fear when trying new things?**

The day I gave my speech to convince everyone in my school to vote for me as secretary of the student council, I was sweating bullets before I even hit the stage. And to make matters worse, when I approached the podium, it was too tall and I couldn't see over it.

Immediately, my insecurities started mounting one by one. They almost got the best of me, but I thought quickly on my feet. I figured, hey, I'm already on this stage, I might as well make the most of it. I got on my tippy toes, took the mic off the podium, moved to the middle of the stage, and used that vertical challenge situation as a little joke to break the ice. And the entire gymnasium laughed!

I used my authentic voice and my petite stature to give the speech of my teenage career. I did what I came to do and took control over what I was able to control. I couldn't control the outcome and I couldn't control my height, but I could tell the audience why I was the one for the job. Even though I was nervous and other kids who were running were more popular than me, I still believed I belonged. And the student body did too: I won the most votes for the position.

Now, think about that for a second. What if I had let my fears suffocate my curiosity to lead? Maybe my courage helped another student who had been questioning themselves as well. Sometimes someone else might be waiting on us to be the role model for resilience so they can see what it looks like.

Tools for Your Tool Kit

We've talked about how sometimes, we get the yes we've been waiting for and other times, our best efforts might not result in a happy ending. No matter what, we can always make the choice to try our best and to make sure we don't beat ourselves up mentally if things don't turn out our way.

My experiences with the cheer squad, the basketball team, and the student council all helped me learn some valuable lessons about life and myself: I learned how to continue on, even if I was feeling disappointed.

I hope you will consider taking some of my advice when you are met with similar situations. Please just promise me that you won't let hearing the word "no" stop you from reaching your finish line.

Before we move on toward the end of this chapter, I wanted to share a few more tips with you on how to reframe future no's. Let's take a look at some scenarios to help paint a better picture:

Being Vulnerable. It hurt when I didn't make the team in both cases, but I also realized that those coaches were looking for something, and if they didn't see what they were looking for in me, that had nothing to do with me. It was about them, and their ideas of putting a team together had nothing to do with my worth.

Sometimes, when we receive a "no" or a "not right now," we tell ourselves that something is wrong with us, when in fact there is nothing wrong. We will just have to take our magic someplace where everyone is fully invested in our success and identity.

In the case of my basketball and cheerleading teams, when the coaches chose such a small number of Black and brown girls—or none—I could see that they weren't committed to fostering a diverse and inclusive squad. I don't want to spend my time convincing anyone that I belong, when all I want to do is play the sport I love.

Perseverance. If I had never received those no's from the cheerleading and basketball coaches, I would never have considered running for student council. And I would have missed out on learning how to be a leader!

Running for student council showed me that I was good at

inspiring other students. And the other skills that I learned enhanced my public speaking and taught me how to run a meeting and how to gain buy-in from others. I might not have learned those skills on the sports teams.

It's easier to feel sorry for yourself than to uplift yourself when you're feeling down, but you never know what other opportunities are waiting for you. And that's why it's so important to use your affirmations when those moments arise!

Managing Expectations. Managing my expectations was extremely important. It's not realistic to expect to go through life never hearing the word "no." I mean, I would hear it a few times a week in my house! Why did I ever think I wouldn't hear it outside of my home?

The reality is, life is filled with yeses, no's, maybe's, and not right nows. And that's okay! You can expect some disappointment, but you have strategies to manage them, and you have tools to help you try again.

The Best Is Yet to Come

As a person who has been where you are now, please trust me when I say things get better.

I have felt the angst you're feeling. Heck, there are times in my adult life that I still might feel that angst.

I also know that you're experiencing so many things for the

first time, and you're learning as you go. As you go through your wins and losses, please know you don't have to endure any of it alone. I hope you will take some of my advice and apply it.

I have one last story to share with you in this chapter: Almost twenty years after I heard all those no's as a teenager, my high school awarded me the Distinguished Alumni Award. I was the first Black woman to receive the award. And when they notified me—wow, I had some big emotions.

I thought back to all those times in school when I felt like not making the team was the end of the world. I thought back to the times I felt like Black wasn't beautiful because those coaches chose white girls with blond and brunette hair over Black girls with braids. I thought back to not seeing my name on the basketball A team list.

But when they notified me of my award, they didn't bring up any of my no's and they didn't remind me of those times I didn't win. All they thought about was my successes. I wish someone had told me at your age what was awaiting me all these years later. And I cry tears of joy, because I get to tell you all these things right now.

I thought back to the little Minda who couldn't see over the podium. I thought back to when I questioned whether I was even up to the task of being on student council. But most importantly, I thank God that I never gave up on me, even when others didn't see me as the obvious winner. And I don't mean to throw any shade to my former classmates, but it's my name that is on that award—not those coaches or cheerleaders, and that makes me feel really good about myself.

But make no mistake: I earned that distinguished award only because I never gave up on myself. What I now know is that it's really what you do after the "no" that truly counts! I was stronger than those no's, and you are too.

Show Me What You're Workin' With

Now it's time to make resilience real. I've given you some examples and ways to think about what parts of life's equation you have control over. Make no mistake: Life will bring you lots of yeses and plenty of no's, but it's how you handle them that counts.

Use this section to reflect and help you think about how to handle rejection, how you will build resilience, and how you will strategize toward the best possible outcome.

1) When was the last time you experienced hearing a no that caused you to question yourself?

2) Knowing what you know now, how would you handle that situation if it happened again?

3) Write down two affirmations—you can personalize the ones I gave you, or come up with your own—to help you have an empire state of mind when you hear news that you weren't expecting.

4) Why do you think listening and responding to our inner voice is so important? And what are the consequences if we don't confront that negative inner talk?

5) What advice would you give to a friend if they started to tell themselves they would never try again?

CHAPTER 4

What About Your Friends

When I look back on my best moments from my teenage years, most of those moments happened because I established some amazing friendships along the way.

When I got my driver's license, the first place I drove to was to pick up my best friend, Mara. We drove around our small town for several hours, just driving and laughing at inside jokes. I'm pretty sure we drove in and out of the McDonald's parking lot at least twenty times. There was no one at that time in my life that I would have wanted to drive around all day with more than her.

When I was in high school, I thought I would never find another friend that understood me as well as Mara did. But when I got to college, I met some new friends, and they later became more like sisters. A good friendship is like a good bowl of soup: nourishing and so comforting.

Even as I was learning to build good relationships with my friends, I was also learning that sometimes you will have to let friendships go when they no longer serve you or align with your values. I don't know how this next chapter will come off to you, but since you've made it to Chapter Four, I feel like we are pretty much family at this point, and I will always commit to keeping it 100 percent real with you. So here it is: I wish someone had told me about the importance of finding and maintaining healthy friendships when I was younger.

Having healthy friendships is not just about finding your BFF. Nor is it just about who wants you to sit at their table during your lunch hour or whether people think you are "popular" or not. If I'd had someone like a big sister to tell me about the importance of having healthy friendships with other girls and with other people in general, I would have made some better friend choices along the way.

Mara and my sister-friends from college are all amazing, but I wasted time with others who weren't worth it. When you're young, no one talks about what it takes to build and maintain good friendships. They just tell you to "make friends." Nor do folks provide you with a road map for when you might have to let some friendships go. But the reality is, some friends will be in your life for a season, reason, or lifetime—you just need to know who fits in which bucket.

And, before I forget, some of you might be thinking, well, I just want some friends that look like me. I understand that sentiment, because when I moved to my small town, I didn't have too many friends that looked like me. When I was in high school, I desperately wanted that as well, because I was always the only Black girl in my friends' circle of mostly white girls.

It wasn't until I went to college that I was able to establish some amazing friendships with other Black and brown girls. Obviously you don't have to make friends only with people who look the way you do, but it's nice to have a more diverse circle of friends—when you are experiencing some of the unique challenges that only Black and brown girls face, you won't feel so isolated.

In this chapter, I'm going to help you learn how to build friendships, identify what a healthy friendship looks like, and better understand when it's time to let some of those friendships go because they no longer align with your values and goals. And lastly, I will share with you how to build a network, because not only do you need good friends in your life, but you need some adults who can be supportive in your future endeavors.

Finding Good Friends

I love a good friendship, especially with other women, and when I was younger, building my girl squad brought me so much joy.

I'm sure when I mentioned my squad, you immediately thought about your squad too. When I was younger, my grandmother said to me, "Minda, when you get to be my age, you will be able to count your good friends on one hand." As a teenager, I thought my grandmother didn't know much about friendships, because at that time, I had more "friends" than I knew what to do with. Or so I thought.

Granny was right: In my adult life, I can count my good

friends on one hand. Now, don't get me wrong, I have tons of people I'm cool with or that I might pop up at their birthday party and celebrate them. But there are only a select few that I trust to have my back through anything.

Often, we put so much pressure on our friendships. I remember agonizing over the thought of not having a best friend like some of my other friends. I felt like all I ever heard other girls say is "My best friend this" or "My best friend that." I used to think something was wrong with me because I didn't have one best friend—I had a few really great friends that I loved.

I never understood the reason why there has to be a "best." And to be honest, I still feel that way. But if you have one, that's an awesome thing too. My only hope is that, by the end of this chapter, building friendships and creating a network won't seem so daunting, because when you have a good squad, there is nothing that compares.

Quick Q's: Have you ever felt the pressure to make new friends? Or do you subscribe to the rapper Drake's philosophy when he said, "No new friends"?

As I mentioned before, friendships can last a season, can be for a reason, or can last a lifetime. I've made friends in all those categories. And if you are blessed enough to experience a good friend in your life, then you are winning. Those lifetime friends are gold. They're the kind you don't have to talk to every day, because a true friendship like yours can survive even when you haven't seen each other in months. And when you do reconnect, it's like you never missed a beat and you can still finish each other's sentences.

But there are some friends who are only for a season or a reason, and talking about those types of friendships can be a little harder. One confusing thing we all feel as we try to make friends is the need to be liked. I think sometimes that feeling gets so strong that we don't always choose the best people to befriend. Sometimes we end up trusting people who have already shown us they'll never be a good friend, but we didn't heed the warning signs because we were listening to that big need to be liked instead of our intuition.

Let me tell you about one of these friendships. I met Candy when I was in the sixth grade. We went to grade school, junior high, and high school together. I gave her chance after chance after chance to be a better friend. And I just kept thinking she would do better each time after her apologies, but it never happened, until I finally had to end that friendship.

Ending a friendship, be it toxic or healthy, hurts no matter what. Yet, if I had ended that toxic friendship years earlier, when I first started seeing signs that Candy couldn't be a good friend to me, it wouldn't have ended so disastrously.

When we first started hanging out in sixth grade, no one could tell me that Candy wasn't my girl! Whenever my parents would say, "Minda, watch out for Candy, I don't know if she's a real friend," I used to think they just didn't understand and were being too old-school about friendships. They would always warn me that she might be using me. At the time, I couldn't see how that was possible, because we had so much fun together. But, if I am being honest with myself, I didn't want to see the red flags, so I ignored them. And eventually, I realized that Candy really was using me.

At that time, Candy would always come over to my house after school. I thought it was because she wanted to hang out with me, but I later found that coming to my house just allowed her to be closer to her boyfriend's house. She was using coming to my house as an excuse to give to her parents. And once she broke up with that boyfriend, she didn't need my house anymore, and she went to the next person and used their house as her excuse.

It took me a while to figure this out. That was the first cycle of Candy's and my toxic friendship, and I could have ended it there, but I didn't. Candy and I remained casual friends because we shared some of the same friends, but we didn't hang out after high school.

Then, after I graduated from college, we reconnected, and I was put right back in the same situation with her again. I had a condo in Chicago, and sometimes I would invite her over, because she was still so much fun to be around. And then I realized that she was trying to use my house as a place to meet up with guys. She might have gotten older, but her values hadn't changed since we were teenagers!

Once I understood that, I knew I had to cut the relationship off once and for all. I refused to continue opening myself up to someone who didn't value my boundaries, and who couldn't be honest and loyal. Once I learned those boundaries through my friend breakup with Candy, I knew I had to apply them to my other friendships.

Learning to build healthy relationships will add value and joy to your friendships and serve you for the rest of your life. Each of us will have friends like Candy, and we'll have to decide how to handle it. I hope you'll be able to see the warning signs earlier than I did!

Maybe you've already found yourself in a similar situation, or maybe you aren't sure what a healthy friendship looks like yet. So here are some ways to identify when a friendship is no longer right for you:

A true friendship won't require you to act like someone else to maintain the friendship. If you find that some of the people you consider your friends ask you to lie for them, or they put you in a situation that could end up with you grounded, you might want to reevaluate that friendship. Because if you were my friend, I'd want us to have fun together, but I wouldn't want us ending up in jail together—you feel me?

True friendship won't feel like you are always trying to prove yourself to them. No real friend will ever say, if you do this for me, then I know you're my friend. That is called manipulation.

For example, imagine your so-called friend says, "If you do my homework for me, I'll make sure I save you a seat at lunch on Friday." That doesn't even seem like a fair exchange, does it? And to be honest, yes, friends do nice things for their friends, but if you find that *you* are always doing and that person is never showing you friendship in return, then that is a one-sided friendship.

Remember my former friend Candy. She only seemed to befriend me when it benefited her the most. When I look back on that friendship, I am not too sure what I ever got out of it.

And lastly, friendship doesn't constantly cause you pain. A friend who constantly talks down to you, makes fun of you, or makes you feel sad after most of your interactions is not really your friend. True friendship is meant to empower you, love you, support you, and inspire you.

Now, I realize that when you're in school, social pressure is at a ten, and all we want to do is make friends. It's normal to want someone to hang out with, go to school dances with, talk to, or go shopping with. It's natural to want to have a squad. I want you to learn how to build a squad that makes you better, and you make them better.

Ultimately, the way you identify, build, and foster relationships with friends will help you navigate other relationships as you mature into adulthood and in your career. Relationship building is a skill set that you will never stop using.

Building Relationships

Now that we've talked about the hard stuff, let's switch gears and talk about what friendship *should* look like.

I love my friends. We laugh together, we shed tears together, and we travel together. But most importantly, we serve as a sounding board for each other in those moments when we need a little perspective. And let's be honest, we all need a strong squad who will help us find some good trouble on a Friday night. My friendships enrich my life, and I hope yours do too.

Remember when I mentioned my best friend from back in the day, Mara? When I met Mara, I was in my first year in high school, and she was a sophomore. Our lockers were near each other and we began to get to know each other. We had this fun little back-and-forth banter, and eventually she invited me to hang out with her and her friends one weekend. And from that first official hang-out, we became the best of friends.

We liked the same shows, we liked the same music, and we loved having fun and laughing. There was nothing that I didn't feel comfortable telling her and vice versa. And there's something else that surprised me about my friendship with Mara—she was a white girl.

I had other white friends before meeting her, of course, but I had never felt a connection like I did with her. That friendship showed me that I could trust girls who don't look like me. Mara was genuine and authentic. I never had to worry about her racially insulting me or culturally appropriating—just the way a friendship should be. And not to mention, my parents never had to warn me about her!

Please don't be afraid to try to make new friends, even if you've had a bad experience like the one I had with Candy. Just because one friendship doesn't work out doesn't mean you should throw away the opportunity to build another one, like the relationship I built with Mara. I am so glad I allowed myself to trust again. And I hope you can allow yourself to trust again and get to know someone new without the baggage of past experiences.

If you experienced a romantic breakup, would you vow to never date again? Of course not, otherwise, you might miss out on your next best thing! Yes, you might take a break from dating, but you wouldn't let your last relationship dictate the rest of your life, would you? No, you would just understand the warning signs and red flags related to why that relationship didn't work out and use that information in your next relationship. Friendship is no different.

So let's dig into the other side of friendship. I want you to know what a healthy and loving friendship can look like:

Friendship is being loyal, respectful, loving, and honest. You need a good girlfriend who will call you out in a loving way when you are feeling yourself too much, and you need a good friend who will hold a secret that it took a lot of courage for you to share. Accountability and love are required in any good friendship or relationship.

Friendship is about the quality and not the quantity. News flash: There is no place on your résumé or in a future interview where you will be asked "How many friends do you have?" Nor will your college application ask you to check a box if you were the most popular kid in your grade. Sometimes we put way too much focus on the wrong aspects of friendship.

Let me ask you a quick question. Would you rather have twenty friends that never know much about you and are never there for you when you really need them? Or would you prefer to have three friends who will ride to the ends of the earth with you? Those three loyal friends know your family and will ask you if you brought your inhaler because they know when you get to laughing, you also start wheezing. Yo . . . those are the kind of friends I want.

And those are the kind of friends I still have! The friend who might even have a rescue inhaler for me in their purse. (Okay, I am being silly, but I think you get my point.) The bottom line is, find you some real ones!

And since we are talking about what good friendships look like, I think it's also important to mention that we don't just want good squad members for ourselves—we should also strive to be a good friend in return. It takes the people on both sides to make a good friendship work!

Unfortunately, there is no class that any of us can take on how to be a good friend. Many of us figured it out or messed up and lost some friends along the way. And some just can't understand how to be a good friend even if you give them a ten-step process. So I hope you will remember that reciprocity—equal give-and-take—is required in any healthy friendship.

Quick Q's: What kind of friend would you say that you are? What are your strengths, and what could you improve on?

Oh, and remember when I mentioned the excitement I felt when I met the Wilson girls? It's also important to befriend other girls that look like us, so that we don't feel so isolated during those times in our lives when we might not have anyone who looks or identifies the way we do in our classrooms or workplaces.

I do believe that as young Black and brown girls, we must learn to be great friends to each other. We must learn to show love to our sister-friends and be there for them when it counts. We don't have to hate on each other, and we don't have to shame one another. There is room for all of us to show that we are more than magic!

And never forget: It's important to be the type of friend that you would want to be a friend to you.

I know you might be wondering why I am focusing so much on friendships. It's because I believe good friendships play such a vital role for Black and brown girls.

Like I said before, if I hadn't met the Wilson girls when I felt the loneliest, I don't know how the rest of my school year might have played out. I told you that eventually they moved to a town farther away, but several years later when I had my driver's license and my own car, we reconnected and were able to visit each other in our high school and college days. And I am happy to report that we remain in touch.

Quick Q's: If you haven't met your "Wilson girls" yet, what organizations or clubs can you join that might provide you the opportunity to make friends that you identify with?

We need good friends that look like we do so we can feel supported in a world that doesn't always highlight and amplify our achievements like it does for other girls. One of my first good friends called me a tar baby and it nearly broke me. It was the first time I experienced a friend breakup, and it hurt. When that situation happened to me, I spent a lot of time feeling mad. I had a hard time understanding how that white girl didn't understand that that type of language was racist! And it sure wasn't the way I want to be treated by anyone that is supposed to be my friend, even if they said they were just joking.

I knew I needed new friends—Black and brown girls whom I could rely on and relate to, and who could help when I felt like some of these majority white spaces were driving me crazy. As an adult, I've thought a lot about the need for Black and brown girls to have friends who look like them in their youth, and how impactful those friendships can be.

One of my younger cousins is about to head off to college this year. She has a small group of friends that love getting together at each other's homes. Sometimes when I call my aunt to check in, all I hear is the girls in the background laughing.

One day, I asked my cousin, "What does it mean to you to have a group of Black and brown girls that you can call your friends during this time in your life?" She told me that two of her close girlfriends had been slated to go off to college the year before, but due to COVID-19, they ended up having to take their classes remotely. Before, she had been so sad that she would no longer have them around and that she might need to find some new friends to hang out with during her last year of high school. This extra time with them had been a relief; she wasn't sure how she would have made it through the pandemic year without such close friends.

Prior to my cousin meeting her friends, she had attended schools where there weren't many girls that looked like her. She admitted that back then, she hadn't realized how much representation mattered, and how nice it was now to not always have to explain everything about being a Black girl to your white friends. She just kept saying, "They get me."

Shortly after our conversation, I started thinking about how happy I was when I got to college and made some amazing friendships with other Black and brown girls. I didn't have the opportunity to build those types of relationships in my small town.

When I was in college, I met two of my sister-friends, Liz and Jamie. Originally, I met Liz casually at a friend's house. Later that school year, we ended up living on the same dorm floor and she introduced me to her best friend Jamie. From that moment forward the three of us were inseparable. Everyone on campus knew we were the three amigas.

Those two girls, some of the best moments in my life were spent with them. If one of us had our last twenty dollars, that meant we split it three ways so we all could benefit from it.

Unfortunately, Liz passed away a couple of years ago and attending her funeral was one of the hardest things I've ever had to do. I flew to Chicago from New York City, drove two hours to pick up my mother, and then we drove another four hours to attend the funeral, only to turn right back around and head home. And those were just the physical hardships of attending Liz's funeral, not to mention the emotional ones.

I had never known a friendship like the one that me, Jamie, and Liz shared until I experienced it. We were three Black girls that understood what it meant to be a Black girl in America, and we supported each other, and reminded one another that we were more than magic even back then! Again, they weren't just my friends, they were my sisters, and I wouldn't trade the love and support we gave each other for anything in this world.

My relationships with Liz and Jamie weren't just about having fun (although we did love coordinating our outfits for parties!). We also shared similar values.

For example, Liz was a pastor's kid and so was I. We were able to bond over some of the strict religious experiences we had growing up, like only being able to listen to gospel music.

And with Jamie, she had a younger brother that she was crazy over, and I have two younger brothers as well and we vibed off being the oldest sisters.

One of my biggest takeaways from my friendship with these two is that when we did have a disagreement or maybe someone was dating a person we didn't approve of, we always made space to speak our truth to one another. We were able to do that because we knew that our advice was always rooted in love and respect. And even when one of us made a mistake, we were always there to have each other's back. That was table stakes—the bare minimum—for us!

I was the oldest of the three of us, and I looked at them like little sisters at times. When I got my apartment off campus, I would have nights where I would cook us a family dinner. And when one of us needed help taking our braids down, we were never shy about asking for help, because that process could take hours. We just got each other.

One more thing about Liz and Jamie: We called ourselves the Silver Dollars. I know you probably want to laugh, but I'm sure your crew has a name too. And the joy I still get when I receive a message from Jamie that says "Hey SD, just thinking about you"—there is no better feeling.

I haven't seen Jamie in a few years, but we maintain the love and the relationship even miles away. Being friends with her and Liz was easy. And that is another point I would like to drive home about healthy friendships: Friendships might take work, but they shouldn't make you miserable. Friendships that are based on love will always help you grow. Those are the types of relationships that I pray you find. And don't settle for anything less.

Remember, if you do get a chance to make friends with girls who look or identify the same as you, you don't have to compete with each other. You don't have to talk bad about each other; you can be supportive and become a squad that gets each other!

Before me and my cousin got off the phone, she told me that she hopes to be able to attend college with one of her girlfriends next year. She also applied to quite a few Historically Black Colleges and Universities (HBCUs), because she wants the experience of being around more people that look like her. And if you are struggling to find other girls that look like you, perhaps choosing to attend a college or university with more Black and brown people might be a good road to explore!

You Know That They're Toxic

One thing I will admit to you is that sometimes people label me as "too nice." And the too nice part of me always wants to give people a first, second, and third chance at the expense of my own well-being. But that's a mistake.

It's one thing to be a nice person, but it's another thing to allow people to mistake your kindness for a weakness. And sometimes, when you are too nice, you want to see the good in everyone. I kept trying to see the good in people like Candy. But when people show you who they are the first time, please believe them, sis!

Maybe you've had some family members try to warn you about some toxic or "bad" friends like my parents tried to do with Candy. And unfortunately, sometimes we don't listen, because we want to see the good in the people we call our friends. I pray to God you don't have to learn the hard way when it comes to friendships, because it ain't worth it, trust me.

There are too many great people out there waiting to show you what good looks like, so why would you want to spend your energy on making friends with people who will only hurt you down the road? I bet if you sit and think about some of the friendships you've had up to this point, you've probably had a Candy or two in your life, and the only question I have to pose to you is, why?

It's important to always ask ourselves these questions: Does this friendship make me a better person? And, can we grow together? If the answer to those questions is no, then it's important to ask yourself another question: Why am I in this friendship at all?

The reason I kept Candy around longer than I should have was probably that she was so much fun to be with. Candy was the life of any party she showed up at! I used to tell myself, well, she's fun, she makes me laugh. But let me tell you, you can watch a comedy show if you want to laugh, but friendship—a real friendship—should be deeper than that. Because Candy caused more pain than laughs. Black and brown girls: I ask you to always choose yourself.

It's a privilege for other people to have someone like you in their life, and you have to act like that's the truth by setting boundaries and choosing your friends wisely.

Draw Your Line

Let me quickly touch on setting boundaries. Much of my friendship with Candy had no boundaries. She knew she could apologize, and I would forgive her. And the moment I finally did create boundaries, she decided she didn't like them and we went our separate ways.

It's almost like that Beyoncé lyric "The first time I say no, it's like I never said yes." The first time I flexed some boundaries you would have thought I committed a crime, the way Candy responded to me. There were so many times I went along with what *she* wanted, but the minute I was honest with her about what *I* wanted from our friendship, she was out the door.

Candy decided our years-long friendship wasn't worth respecting my boundaries, and it hurt. But I was glad I was honest with her, because her leaving gave me more time and energy to make new friends and focus on the relationships that made me feel good, the ones with equal give-and-take. You should always be able to be honest with your friends and they should always give you the benefit of the doubt. It doesn't mean you will always agree, but you will seek to find a resolution that benefits you both.

You might be thinking, okay, I understand that sometimes we need to establish and stand firm with the boundaries we set, but that sounds easier said than done, Minda. And that is why I wrote this book, so we could discuss things like this!

First things first: I can't tell you what boundaries you should set. That depends on your comfort level. You have to first understand what sits well with you and what doesn't. Instead, I would like to present to you two steps you might consider taking to help you establish and maintain boundaries with your friends. (And, just so you know, setting boundaries isn't just for toxic friendships. Establishing boundaries will help you maintain your healthy relationships too.)

Figuring Out Your Comfort Level. It's important for you to understand what makes you feel alive when you're around your friends, and when you get a feeling that trouble might be around the corner. I'm sure you've felt both emotions depending on which friend you're spending time with.

For example, growing up, I was very petite. And, because I was so much smaller than my friends, starting when I was in grade school, many of them thought it was cute to try to pick me up like I was some kind of baby doll. No one ever asked permission, and I absolutely hated it!

Back then, I felt like I couldn't say anything because I didn't want anyone to think I was being rude. And even in college, I had one guy pick me up and accidentally drop me. I knew what my comfort level was—having both feet planted on the floor—but I hadn't figured out how to communicate it yet.

Say What You Mean, Without Saying It Mean. Even though my friends always meant well, that didn't change the fact that I don't like being picked up. That's why I needed to establish this boundary.

Regardless of their intention, it made me feel uncomfortable, and I didn't think it was appropriate for people to be picking me up without my permission. And the moment my football player friend accidentally dropped me, I was so mad, I went bananas! He had never seen me get so mad before. And because he saw how it made me feel, and he didn't want to hurt me, he never tried it again.

Come to think about it, no one has tried to pick me up ever since, because I established HARD boundaries around my personal space and comfort level. Perhaps if I had been clear about not wanting to be picked up sooner, so many people wouldn't have continued to try to do it. I felt like I couldn't say anything, when in fact, we always have a right to choose our comfort over anyone else's.

We all have our own boundaries, and you shouldn't feel

apologetic for telling one of your friends how you feel. Let's say you don't like people hugging on you—it's important that you learn to establish that boundary up front so that you don't go the rest of your life feeling uncomfortable with every interaction with your friends.

When a friend tries to give you a hug even though hugging isn't your cup of tea, you can always say what you mean, without saying it mean. It might go something like this: "I realize you like to hug, but hugging isn't really my thing; maybe we can do a fist bump instead?" Now, maybe you don't want to do a fist bump either, but I think you get my drift.

Setting boundaries is about centering yourself. Boundaries are meant to help you make a commitment to yourself about what you feel is appropriate and what doesn't fly with you. Some people might not get it right the first time, but you can continue to draw your line and set your boundaries, because eventually, they will learn how to engage with you in ways that make you feel comfortable.

Part of being a good friend is making sure we are not making our friends uncomfortable, even if we don't intend to make them feel uncomfortable. A real friend would want to know what makes you happy and what makes you sad, and they would want you to establish boundaries so that you can have a healthy and happy friendship. And any so-called friend that has a problem with you speaking your truth—well, that might not be a friendship worth fighting for!

Squad Up

In this chapter, I have mentioned the word "squad" a time or two. A squad is essentially your friend group. I think it's important to build a squad that's right for you.

I'm not writing this because I want to choose your friends for you. I'm telling you this because I want you to understand how important your relationships are even at your age. I want you to be able to find people to add to your squad whose values are similar to yours.

And since I brought up values, what are *your* values when it comes to having healthy friendships with other people? Do you like friends who are loyal, trusting, and family-oriented? If your answer was yes, then those might be some values that you look for in people that you want to bring into your friend circle.

For example, one of my core values is kindness. Being a kind and thoughtful person means a lot to me. That's why I always try to fill up my squad with kind people!

I have never been a fan of hanging out with mean girls. My friends weren't the girls who were making fun of other girls at school or causing unnecessary drama. I am not saying I was a perfect teenager, but there were certain people I could be friendly with, yet they wouldn't be girls you would find me hanging out with on a Friday night. Because you know what— mean girls turn into mean women in college and in the workplace, and I ain't got time for that.

Plus, why would you want to hang out with girls who sit

around and talk mess about other girls behind their backs? And why would you want to be friends with girls who are friends with you one day and the next they don't even invite you to their birthday party? Like come on, sis, do you think those types of friendships last? I think we both know the answer to that—so it's better to understand what type of friendships will serve you and which ones will only cause you pain.

The friends I have as an adult are like sisters, and I am able to maintain those relationships because I've also learned what it takes to be a good friend in return. Through many years of experience, I have learned what type of friend I want to be and what type of friend I want to have. And when you find good friends, you do what you gotta do to maintain those relationships.

I make sure to ask myself, how can I still show up for my friends when we no longer live in the same state? And how can I continue to be a good friend when we get married and some of us have kids, and we don't have the time to hang out like we once did? Life happens, and friendships look different at different times in our lives. But even as we've gotten older and our lives have gotten busier, my friends and I can still be good friends to one another by making the conscious choice to prioritize our friendship.

Listen, I want you to find some amazing squad members. I want you to have friends you can travel with and go to football games with—but I don't want you to want to make friends so badly that you forfeit the values that matter to you. Finding your best friend forever doesn't have to be your goal—your goal should be building healthy friendships that inspire and make you better, with you providing that same level of friendship in return.

Now our friendships can be maintained from anywhere in the world because of the power of technology. When I was around your age, we had limited access to the Internet and text messaging was not a thing, so we had to call our friends on the phone or write and mail off a letter that would arrive at their home in a few days. One of my really great childhood friends went to a different high school from me, but we maintained our relationship by hanging out on the weekends and staying connected in the ways that we could.

Friendship doesn't have to be defined by how often you talk or what that person does for you. It's more important to think about the ways you add value to each other's lives—that should always be the goal. And when we learn how to maintain healthy relationships with people, we can repeat that behavior in our jobs and other places that we interact with others.

Your Network

So far we've discussed healthy and unhealthy friendships. As you continue to get older you will learn that making friends doesn't stop when you graduate school. You'll also make friends at work. This is called networking or relationship building.

Many of the ideas we've talked about around making friends are also important to keep in mind as you start building work relationships. You'll want to be aware of what boundaries you want to set, and you'll want to think about whether the new people you meet have the same values you do.

When I was seventeen years old I took a job at a pet food store. The woman who owned it was amazing. Her name was Tiffany, and I was so smitten by how smart and driven she was at twenty-seven years old, and she seemed like such a BOSS.

When you live in a small town, you don't come across women like her every day. You only read about boss ladies like her in magazines and see them on television. Tiffany had a really nice home on the lake and she was making major moves as a business owner. She gave me a snapshot of the type of working woman I hoped to grow into someday.

When I began working with Tiffany, she taught me so much about business and how to engage with the customers that came into the store by providing great customer service. I learned about building good working relationships so that new customers would turn into returning customers. When I left that job to go away to college, I knew that Tiffany was someone I wanted to keep in contact with. I wanted her to remain in my squad in some way. So I stayed connected with her and periodically I would call her, email, and use social media to keep in touch.

Fast-forward ten years, and I was twenty-seven years old living in Los Angeles, California. Tiffany and her family were living in Arizona, and she invited me to fly out for the weekend and stay in her guest house. I felt comfortable doing that, because even though I hadn't seen her in over ten years, we'd maintained our relationship.

If you had asked me at seventeen whether I'd still be in touch with Tiffany at twenty-seven years old, my hope was that I could say yes. But in order to build relationships and maintain them, it requires some intentionality and work. And when I think back to when Tiffany hired me, I had no idea that our relationship would grow into what it became. Friendship tends to sometimes happen that way—you never know where that friendship will lead to.

The unique part about the friendship I had with Tiffany is that our initial relationship was not a friendship, but a manager-employee relationship. As we got to know each other better, we began to build a sense of trust. She began to invite me to her home and I even babysat her young son, Trey, a time or two.

Tiffany was a savvy businesswoman and I too wanted to be a businesswoman when I grew up. She taught me a lot about being unapologetically driven even at a young age. She taught me that if you work hard, you can have nice things. I was able to ask her for advice and learn how to run a business.

Tiffany became my mentor, and I became her mentee. A mentor is someone who can give you advice. A mentor tends to be someone who is not in your friend group. For example, maybe you have someone who has helped you prep for an interview. Or perhaps you've asked someone you trust for financial advice. The advice givers that are invested in us living our best lives tend to serve as formal and informal guides or mentors.

And you should definitely have one of those people for your squad.

> *Quick Q's*: Do you have any relationships with adults or role models that remind you of my relationship with Tiffany? Any teachers, coaches, or friends' parents who are invested in your well-being? If so, they might be people you continue to stay in contact with.

Now that you get the importance of relationship building, let's talk about how you build a network that you can leverage throughout your life. Some of the relationships you're building now are helping you build your future network, and you'll continue to add to your squad (network) along the way. I know Drake said no new friends, but trust me, you will need a few more at various times in your life.

I used the example of my relationship with Tiffany to show you how relationships with adults sometimes take time to grow and how important it is to have a good network beyond your peers. Tiffany and I stayed in touch over the years, and I continued to benefit from having this relationship that I created while I was in high school. The fun part of growing your network like this is that you never know when you might need their help or when you might be helpful to them down the line.

. . .

Here's another example of building my network: When I graduated from college, I had a professor I'd taken about three or four courses with for my women's studies minor. Because I saw her so often, I began to engage with her before and after class, and she began to get to know me a little better than some of her other students. When I decided to apply to graduate school, on the application I had to have a couple of recommendations from past teachers. Thankfully, I had a relationship with my professor, and I was able to ask her if she would consider writing a recommendation for me even two years after I had graduated from undergrad.

It might have been extremely awkward for me to reach out to her and ask for such a personal request if she only got to know me because of seeing my name on the papers she graded. It would have been hard for her to speak to my character as a student or give reasons as to why I should be accepted into this program, if she never got to know me in a real way.

And let me tell you, as a professor now myself, I appreciate the students who ask for my help when they have actually created a relationship with me during the times they had me as a teacher. Even years later, some of my past students send me messages updating me on how life after college is for them. The reality is, maybe I will never see those students again, but I am now in their network and they are in mine, because we continue building our relationship.

And that is how you identify and continue to build relationships with people who you think add value to your life. There is so much overlap between building a network with people you bring into your life through work and school, and building a solid group of friends. In both cases, you want to build a squad of people that are invested in your success and you in theirs.

Mentorship

Some of the people in your network might become mentors for you, just like Tiffany was for me.

But mentorship doesn't always have to come from someone you know in real life. There are so many people that I consider mentors even though I've never met them. For example, I like to listen to a lot of financial podcasts. Many of those podcast hosts probably don't even know that I exist, yet their content and advice have helped me make better financial decisions.

You might find mentors through listening to podcasts, attending workshops, or even reading this book. I might be serving as a mentor to you right now, and we've probably never met!

You can have more than one mentor. I have probably five or six mentors that I go to for advice on different parts of my life. It's important that you maintain those mentorship relationships just as you would a close friendship. You don't want the person who is giving you advice to feel like you only come to them when you need something.

I have another mentor I'd like to tell you about named Barry. I met Barry at a fundraising event for a nonprofit organization that we both supported. Barry became a mentor to me much later in my career.

At one point in my life, my work would take me to the San Francisco area at least twice a month. And on some of those visits, I would schedule time to grab coffee with Barry and we would catch up on what was going on in my life and his, and maybe strategize on the next steps in my career. Eventually, I changed jobs and I no longer was visiting San Francisco as often. So that meant I didn't get to have those face-to-face opportunities with Barry like I once did.

I truly valued the advice and relationship I was building with Barry and at first, I worried that our mentor/mentee relationship would end because I wasn't able to visit with him anymore. But one thing I want you to know is this: Just because you aren't able to be in the same room with someone, doesn't mean you can't continue building your relationship and receiving advice from them. It just means that your communication styles might have to change, but the relationship can still flourish.

I ended up scheduling phone calls or video chats with Barry once or twice a year so we could maintain our relationship. Additionally, I would send him and his wife holiday cards when appropriate. And because we stayed connected, our relationship continued to grow.

It's been a couple of years since I've been able to see Barry in person, yet our relationship has grown enough that if I needed to call him right now, he would make time for me. Again, I don't only reach out to him when I need some advice, I also call to check in and send well wishes too. I want to be a good friend in this relationship, just as I would with one of my girlfriends.

You probably have mentors right now and you didn't even realize it. I'm sure that some of your teachers or a coach or a friend's parent has served in this capacity. And at some point you will serve as a mentor for someone else too. If you're hearing really great advice from your mentors, think about sharing it with your friends as well. Some of your friends might not have the privilege of those great mentorship relationships, and you can lift as you climb.

I've said it before: Success is not a solo sport. And when we have access to opportunities and good advice, it's important that we share it with our sisters. Maybe they haven't found their mentor yet, but that doesn't mean they can't thrive and grow too. You will find that not all Black and brown girls will have the same access to opportunities, colleges and universities, and mentors, so try to be conscious of how you can provide that value for them as their friend. You can be a mentor too.

I want to share some tips on how you can engage with a mentor, once you've found one, to make sure you are both getting what you need out of the mentor/mentee relationship, and so you are prepared to maximize your time together:

Be Prepared. When you meet with your mentor, ask yourself, what is it that you want to get out of your time together? Come with a few questions to help guide the conversation. If you were planning a meeting with your boss, would you show up to that meeting with no agenda? You would probably have a few notes written of things you wanted to cover in that meeting. And if you really wanted to have a productive meeting, you would send your questions ahead of time. Remember to give your mentor the same courtesy.

Let your mentor know what your short- and long-term goals are for the next year. They won't be able to help you in the ways you need if you aren't clear on some of your current or future endeavors. For example, maybe you're struggling with deciding which colleges to apply to, and you want them to help you work through it. I want you to be able to take full advantage of the time you have with them to do so.

It's a privilege to have someone you can lean on for advice, so make sure you are respecting the time they give to you. They will thank you for it, and you will have a much more productive conversation.

Remain Flexible and Provide Feedback. Your mentor's time is valuable, and remember, it's yours. Make the most of your meeting by doing research beforehand. That way, you don't leave your meetings feeling frustrated or confused about your next steps. Also, be willing to tell your mentor about what progress you've made, what's worked, and what hasn't. That will allow your mentor to provide feedback on some next steps you can take based on your previous actions, and will allow them to direct you down a different path if necessary.

Maybe you've already found that when you have targeted questions to ask your mentor, those sessions are the most productive for you. It's okay to let them know you like that format. Or, maybe you used to meet once a month but now you'd like to check in twice a month during internship application season. It's okay to ask for some additional time because you have a specific need during a specific period of time, with the understanding that they may or may not say yes depending on how busy they are.

Don't Forget to Give Back. Your mentors can learn from you too! If you're able to, find out how you can support them in their own endeavors. Maybe you can make an introduction or share something new you've learned. Of course, there may be situations where you don't have anything to share and, in this case, consider ways you can pay it forward to others. Or, if you have done a good job of maintaining a long-term relationship with your mentor, you may find a way in the future to give back to them. Keep in mind that a good relationship shouldn't just be a one-way thing.

Those are just a few of the strategies that will help you continue to build and maintain relationships with your current or future mentors. And don't forget to thank them. There's nothing like having a squad of people who are invested in your success, and you don't ever want them to feel like you are taking their time and advice for granted.

I serve as a mentor to a lot of women of color, and I love it when they follow up with me to share how our latest conversation helped them, or what steps they've taken to get closer to their goal. I hate it when people just reach out to me and ask for advice and then never let me know what happened after I gave it. And then the next time they reach out, they just ask for more advice. It feels like a one-sided relationship, and no one likes that!

And just like a friendship, a mentorship relationship might not last forever, and that's okay. I've had mentors that I've kept in touch with for decades. I've had other mentors that gave me advice only when we worked together, but I can hold on to the advice I've received from them for a lifetime. Mentors can be any gender or any age. You should have some mentors that look like you and some that don't. Mentors from all kinds of diverse backgrounds have impacted my life.

As you think about the relationships in your life, remember to ask yourself which ones are working for you, and which aren't. Set the boundaries you need for healthy relationships. Look for mentors who can help you grow. Be honest about yourself and don't be afraid to question whether your relationships are still serving both of you.

Show Me What You're Workin' With

Now it's time to reflect on your relationships. I've given you some things to consider when you are building your squad and finding new mentors. Use this section to reflect and think about what friendship means to you.

1) How will you grow the relationships you want to make stronger?
2) What values are important to you as you maintain relationships?
3) What traits or characteristics do you want to avoid in your friends?
4) What do you think a toxic friendship looks like?
5) Have you ever had a toxic friendship? How did it make you feel?
6) What type of mentor do you think would be helpful to you right now?
7) How will you find these mentors, and how will you continue relationship building with the mentors you already have?

CHAPTER 5

Let's Work

When I was your age, I used to say, "I can't wait until I am an adult."

At that time, being an adult meant staying up all night and buying and doing whatever I wanted. In my imagination, it didn't come along with bills and working forty-plus hours a week. Now that I'm grown, I'm still not excited about paying bills—but I was very excited to get my first adult paycheck.

When I was a teenager, I worked various odd jobs because I liked having money in my pocket. (And for you, I bet you like having money in your Cash App or Venmo account.) For a while I babysat for various families, as if I had my own Babysitters Club of one.

I liked the idea of being quasi-independent. I was really excited when I got my own private phone line for my bedroom. Today, many of our homes don't have a landline at all, because everyone now uses a cell phone. But imagine living in a house with five people and only having one phone!

At that time in my life, I welcomed paying my own telephone

bill each month. I could use the phone whenever I wanted, and I got some independence from providing for myself. Having a part-time job allowed me to purchase some of the extra things that my parents didn't prioritize, like my own phone.

My First Real Job

In this chapter we are going to discuss the rules of engagement around your first job and jobs you might work part-time while you're still going to school. And hopefully, the lessons you learn now will help you later in life as well.

When I was in high school, many of my friends were playing sports after school and your girl was working her fifteen-hour-a-week job so I could have the things I felt were important for a high school girl to have. At first, like I mentioned before, I was babysitting. But you can learn pretty quickly what you like and what you don't like when you work a job. Turns out, working with children is not really my thing. I wanted a job other than babysitting so badly that I begged my parents to let me get a worker's permit. (Fourteen- and fifteen-year-olds need a permit to work in most states.)

Once I got my worker's permit, my friends and I all applied at Dairy Queen. This particular Dairy Queen mostly served ice cream. The girls took care of the ice-cream–related orders and managed the cash register while the guys cooked on the grill. (Now that I think about it, I guess the patriarchy and imposed gender norms in the workplace were at play even in that fast-food job.) But to be honest, I didn't want to cook on the grill, so Blizzards were fine by me.

At any rate, working at Dairy Queen was fun because my friends were all there. We would screw up Blizzard orders and laugh it off. No one took themselves too seriously because we had each other.

But even though we weren't taking ourselves seriously, we should have taken our jobs seriously. I didn't stay at the DQ for too long, but that was one of the most important work lessons I learned there. When some of my friends got fired for joking around too much at work, it was a wake-up call. I was trying to save money to help buy a car when I got my license. I didn't want to have a job just for fun, I wanted a job to help me attain my goals.

The DQ job also gave me the opportunity to learn what type of work I liked and didn't like at an early age. For example, working the cash register was not for me, because it made me anxious having to figure out how much change to give the customer back. I would be sweating bullets when the customer's order cost $7.48 and they would give me a 20-dollar bill. Those cash registers didn't tell you the amount of change to give, and it would take me a minute to do the math in my head. Let me tell you, technology has come a mighty long way!

Handling money was not my thing. (Now, spending it—that I can do!) Any time I could volunteer to work in another station, I jumped at the chance. But the part of that job that I did enjoy was meeting new people as they came in. I really liked talking to customers and seeing how happy they were after I gave them their favorite flavors or snacks. That helped me think about what I wanted from my next job: less math, more personal interaction.

Quick Q's: Have you had some experiences that have shown you what type of work you enjoy doing? For example, maybe you've noticed that you really like working in groups on assignments, or you prefer working on projects independently.

One of my early volunteer jobs was as a helper at a hospital. I would run errands between different departments and answer phones. One of my favorite parts of that job was sitting at the reception desk and helping people when they were lost. I also loved visiting with elderly patients, sitting and talking with them to keep them company. I really enjoyed that.

Another job I had later on was working at the grocery store, and again, I loved the part about helping customers and talking to people, but I didn't like pushing carts in the cold, in the rain, and in the snow. And one time they asked if I wanted to be trained as a cashier and I couldn't say no fast enough. I was triggered from my Dairy Queen cashier days. No thank you!

I'd encourage you to try new things, and lean into the activities you enjoy. There's an old saying: Do what you love, and you'll never work a day in your life. That's not quite true—work is work, no matter how you slice it! But if you have to work, you should try to find the tasks that you enjoy. That will help you on the days when you have to do the parts of the job that aren't as much fun.

Integrity

Now, "integrity" is one of those words that people throw around, and I'm not so sure everyone knows what it means.

My definition of integrity is being honest, having values, and maintaining those values whether people are around you or you are alone. And as a side note—if your integrity is a little shaky, this is a great time to start figuring out what your values are. We've talked about having relationships that align with your values, and if you don't have any, then that could be a problem. But you are more than magic, so I know, homegirl, you got some values!

When I was a teenager, I worked hard to live my values, but I didn't always succeed. When I was working at Dairy Queen, there were so many possible distractions that if I wasn't careful, I could get in trouble with my manager, because he expected me to be working, not joking around with my friends. And he expected that whether he was around or not. If he saw me goofing off, he could fire me. But the only thing that stopped me from goofing off when he *wasn't* around was my own integrity.

In my senior year of high school, I got my first office job. I was hired to assist at this check collection agency. There were times when things at the office were slow and I would finish up early with my calls and letters to people who needed to pay their bills. And instead of asking my manager if she wanted me to help with something else, I would call my friends on the phone. For months, no one said anything to me. And in my opinion, it never interfered with my work. But I had one coworker who noticed, and she ended up reporting me to my manager.

I was called into the CEO's office and he gave me a stern talking-to. I admitted that I had been using the phone to talk to my friends, but I wanted to make it clear that I always got my work done first. I apologized and then went to the bathroom and cried.

It was the first time I cried at work. And it's funny because even telling you this story, I still feel bad about it. Looking back, I think I cried because I was accused of not taking my job seriously. The issue was, I didn't know what I was doing was wrong and my manager didn't care to hear what I had to say about it. Additionally, I was a little ticked off at my coworker who could have come to me first. Both of these adults could probably have used the advice I'll give you in the next chapter about having tough conversations.

I honestly didn't think I was doing anything wrong, and I didn't know that I should have asked for more work. I thought that since I was done with what I was assigned to do, I could do other things. I wasn't trying to be sneaky or get over on anyone,

I just didn't know! My coworker was a full-time employee who could have mentored me and helped me, but instead, she chose to paint a much uglier picture of my work ethic.

Ultimately, though, I learned a great lesson that day. Even though I felt betrayed by my coworker, because she wasn't perfect either, I still had to own my actions. The CEO didn't call her into the office, he called me.

And if you don't care about any of the lessons that I give you, please take this one to heart: You can't worry about what others are doing, you have to do what you are hired to do—that is where your integrity comes into play. From that day forward, I always erred on the side of asking for more work if I finished my duties earlier than expected. Lesson learned!

Don't Forget the Balance

One thing I learned after that hard lesson at the collection agency is to find a balance.

After I received my stern talking-to, I immediately jumped into the deep end of the pool and started to do everything, just to prove that I wasn't who they tried to paint me to be at that moment, and that I was in fact a very hard worker. I even ended up doing work that I wasn't being paid to do. I just wanted to please everyone in the workplace.

I believe it's important to remember that you can be a go-getter and go after all the things your heart desires. But please don't forget that you don't have to be all the "things" at the expense of stressing yourself out and not giving yourself some grace in the process to grow, breathe, and learn from the mistakes you might make along the way. Always remember that you are human too!

Who Do I Want to Be?

Working at the collection agency was a job I had as I was leaving high school and entering college. It was the first job I actually had to dress up for. It involved a lot of difficult conversations.

Working at the collection agency taught me empathy. Some people would write checks to local businesses and those checks would bounce. Bouncing a check means you don't have the money in your bank account to cover it. If someone bounced a lot of checks, their name would be sent to a collection agency and someone like me would call them on the phone.

On that call, I would tell them to come pay the check amount, plus all the fees they were now being charged because of that one bounced check. Sometimes the check they wrote would be for five dollars, but the bounced check fees would be several times that amount. Their five-dollar check could turn into five hundred dollars, once all the fees were added.

And that isn't the worst part. Some of those businesses would put the person's picture or the bounced check by the cash registers so that no one would let them try to write another check again.

God, why did I ever take that job? As I tell you about it, it sounds so awful. But even at that job, I learned a valuable lesson.

By the time I took that job, I already knew that I liked talking with customers and getting to know people at work. When I called some of the people who wrote those checks, I learned that not everyone wrote "bad" checks because they wanted to scam the system. Sometimes they had lost their jobs or were just trying to make ends meet.

In that job, I learned to hear people out. I learned who I wanted to be in the workplace. I learned that two things can be true at the same time. That I needed to collect their fees, but I could also be kind, empathetic, and treat people with dignity, no matter what. And in every job I held going forward, that lesson was important to me.

What Do I Like Doing?

I learned a little bit about what type of work I like through my high school jobs, but by the time I graduated from college, I still didn't know exactly how to choose my career.

Here are some questions I wish I had known to ask myself back then. I've designed them to help you figure out your own career path:

- **What makes you come alive?**
- **What frustrates you the most?**

- What ideas are you passionate about?
- What do you value?
- What do you think your talents are?
- What impact do you want to make in your career?

Need an example? Here's how I would answer these questions myself.

- **What makes you come alive?** Helping others makes me come alive.
- **What frustrates you the most?** I get most frustrated when I am not acknowledged for my contributions.
- **What ideas are you passionate about?** I'm passionate about making sure no one is treated unfairly. I don't want that for anyone.
- **What do you value?** I value honesty, integrity, and vulnerability.
- **What do you think your talents are?** I think I am talented in public speaking, storytelling, and being empathetic.
- **What impact do you want to make in your career?** I want to help create more opportunities for women of color in the workplace.

Those are my answers, but they're just mine. Only you can decide what the right answers are for you. Not me, not your family or friends—just you. That is part of self-advocacy: You can better advocate for yourself when you know what your WHY is and what YOU want.

Negotiation 101

Now that you've scratched the surface of the *what* and *why* of your career, it's time to start thinking about the *how*.

Let's talk about two more pieces of the career puzzle, starting with negotiation. Immediately, your mind might go to salary negotiation and other money questions. But I'm willing to bet that you've done some negotiation already, both related to money and not.

Perhaps you've asked your parent or guardian if you could stay out a little bit past your curfew. Or maybe you normally get an allowance of twenty dollars per week, but one week you asked for twenty-five because you needed a little extra for popcorn, candy, and soda when you went to see a movie with your friends. You probably didn't realize it, but you were negotiating.

Having savvy negotiation skills will help you no matter where you are in life. It goes back to self-advocacy: If you don't ask for what you want, then how will you ever get it? The part of the equation that is within your control is what *you* do. We might not be able to control the outcome, but at least we can try to change the status quo.

Like you, I first learned to negotiate by asking for what

I wanted from my family and friends. It wasn't too hard. But when it came time to advocate for myself at work and at school, I was facing a much bigger challenge. For example, three months after I graduated from college, I got my first salaried job and signed a lease on my own apartment. The apartment was $600 a month, and that did not include utilities. When I got hired for the job, they offered me $28,000 a year. I knew that I needed at least $30,000 to cover my new expenses for the apartment, gas to get to work, food, and occasional nights out with friends (remember, this was a while back, so you might want a higher salary than that when you graduate).

In negotiations, it's important to recognize your worth. Yes, we should be grateful for what we have—but it's possible to be grateful and still expect better! I was grateful for the job offer and for the starting salary of $28,000, but I also knew that I deserved a job that would pay all of my bills. I noticed that the salary range was $28,000 to $31,000. Even though I didn't have a lot of experience with office jobs, I believed that my high school jobs and the leadership opportunities I had taken in college qualified me for the higher end of the salary range.

I decided to ask for what I needed. I didn't know what the answer would be, but it would be an automatic no if I didn't try to negotiate a higher salary. This conversation would be more complicated than asking my parents for a few more dollars on my allowance, but I used the same skills.

Practicing with family and friends made it easier for me to take on this higher-stakes negotiation. I was clear and confident with the hiring manager, and in the end, they gave me the

$30,000 I needed and I was able to pay my living expenses more comfortably. I was much more satisfied with my work because I knew that I was getting paid fairly.

Let's imagine for a minute that the hiring manager had said no to my request, but that I still wanted to take the job. I would still have been glad I had the conversation for two reasons: First of all, it's better to know for sure than to wonder! And second, I could take the opportunity to plan out my next steps and get that salary increase in the future. I could ask my manager what I needed to do within the next six months to earn a promotion or raise. Once I'd achieved those goals, I could ask again, armed with new evidence for my negotiation.

I know that just reading about negotiation might scare you, but I believe in you and your ability to advocate for yourself. You are the architect of your life. You have the power to build success, and that means having conversations that position you closer to your goals.

Always remember, YOU are your best advocate. Don't sell yourself short!

Practice Makes Perfect

By now you know that I love a good example, so let's test out some script options that you can edit to make them more relevant to your situation.

I am going to give you two examples of what negotiation might look like now and in the future. As I mentioned before, not every negotiation is about money, but learning how to negotiate now will help you in your job and in your everyday life.

Let's say that you turned in an assignment to your teacher or professor. You followed the instructions to the best of your ability, but during class you noticed that many of your classmates interpreted the assignment in a different way. After class, you keep batting around the question in your mind: Did you do the assignment wrong? What will that mean for your grade?

You have two choices: You could do nothing and drive yourself crazy with your woulda, coulda, shouldas about the assignment. Or you could email your teacher, let them know what happened, and advocate for yourself.

Before you send that email, let's come up with a negotiation strategy. You completed the assignment and turned it in on time, so your conscientiousness will work in your favor and might be something to lean into. You're not sure whether you did it wrong, so you could begin by telling the teacher what you're worried about and ask for a clarification. Let's start there.

You email the teacher explaining what you think might have happened. Unfortunately, they tell you you're right: You did do the assignment wrong, and your grade will be lower because of it. This is not the end of the negotiation!

Now that you know all the facts, you can ask for what you need. You email your teacher back to ask whether they would consider allowing you to redo the assignment, or if you could complete another project for extra credit. The teacher might say no, but they might say yes. And don't you believe you are worth finding out what's possible? That is the only part of this equation you have control over. And quite frankly, what do you have to lose?

This is just one way of thinking about negotiations. Let's shift into a salary negotiation. And before you say, "Well, I know they're going to say no, so I won't even bother," or "This isn't a real job," stop! Those phrases should not be in your vocabulary. It's not about them, this is about you!

Unless you have a crystal ball and you have all the answers, you owe it to yourself to ask. You have to be ready for whatever answer they give you, but if you never try to negotiate, then the answer will always be no. And you don't want to leave a possible yes on the table, do you? I didn't think so. Again, what do you have to lose? You have potentially so much more to gain when you bet on yourself.

Now that you have decided you want to negotiate, your next step will require you to do some research. Let's take the fast-food industry for example.

If you're applying for a job, you can use the Internet to search out the hourly wages employers are offering. Maybe you're thinking about applying at McDonald's, In-N-Out Burger, and Shake Shack. Let's say, once you've done your research, you find that (on average) McDonald's cashiers make around $9 an hour, Shake Shack cashiers make $9.61 an hour, and In-N-Out cashiers make $11.13 an hour.

Then let's say one of these establishments offers you $8 per hour. Since you've done your research, you know that most of them are paying their cashiers significantly more than that. If you accepted their $8 per hour offer, you'd be selling yourself short.

You can say something like, "I'd like to discuss that compensation offer and bring it more in line with the market rate in [your city]." Research, research, research! It's the best way to build evidence and make your case. Not to mention, it will signal to them that you came to slay!

The Wage Gap

I have been in the workforce for a while now, and I've known for a long time that women make about eighty-two cents for every dollar a man earns. But when I learned that women of color make less than white women, even when we are doing the same job, I was extremely disappointed.

These discrepancies are called the wage gap. Women who identify as Black, brown, or Indigenous make anywhere from forty-eight cents to sixty-three cents on the white man's dollar.

I know you're probably thinking, "How is this even possible, that isn't fair!" You're right, it's not fair, and women like me are trying to fight for equal pay for equal work so that we all benefit. You can help: Every time you negotiate for more or ask for more, you're decreasing that wage gap. If every woman of color negotiates her salary or other benefits like extra vacation days, we can fix this problem. But if we never advocate for ourselves, we hurt not only ourselves, but the future generations of women of color that would benefit from our courage.

It's Not the End of the World

Before we end our discussion around negotiating and asking for what you want, let's talk about the no's.

In the previous chapter, I mentioned keeping your empire state of mind and not adopting an enemy state of mind when things don't go as planned. So what if you do all of your research and you practice like crazy and still receive a no?

Let me be the first to tell you, it's not the end of the world. It definitely might feel like it, but you did your part. And I think you should still celebrate when you take a step outside of your comfort zone.

If you are met with a no to your request, think about how you can redirect that no. A couple of questions you can ask yourself:

- Is this a definite no or can I come back and ask again later?
- If I wasn't provided a reason as to why I received a no, would I like to ask for further clarification?

Let's take the example I gave earlier: asking your teacher if you can re-do the assignment. Your teacher might flat out say no. And, you might be thinking, why can't I have a chance to turn in a better version of the assignment? One way to handle this is by acknowledging that you respect the decision your teacher has made, but you would like to discuss it further to understand why they made this decision, because you are a stellar student (and your grades reflect it) and this is the first time this has happened.

Now, let's be honest, the situation might not change, but you are asking for some additional clarification to better understand how they landed on this decision. Full stop—some adults might view this as you are stepping out of line or questioning their authority, but that just means they might not understand how to have productive and solution-based conversations, like you are learning to do.

At the end of the day, you can choose what you say and how you want to say it, respectfully. You might be met with more no's, but you might also walk away feeling better, understanding why you received the no. Whatever you decide, I hope this helps you work through those "no's" during your next negotiation!

Show Me What You're Workin' With

Now it's time to reflect on the career-building ideas and negotiation skills we've talked about in this chapter. Use these questions to help you think about your future work and how you can be your own best advocate.

1) What was one project or job you've done in the last year that has brought you joy?
2) What values are most important to you in your work?
3) What is one step you will take to become a better advocate for yourself?
4) How will you respond the next time you ask for what you want, and it doesn't go as you planned?
5) Why do you think self-advocacy is important at work and school?

CHAPTER 6

Tough Conversations

When I was younger, it was really hard for me to have tough conversations.

I didn't like the idea of confronting people when they did something I didn't agree with or were insensitive to my lived experience. Because those conversations made me uncomfortable, I usually just wouldn't deal with them at all. Confrontation was something I would run far away from if I could. But when you don't address things that are bothering you, the problem might grow, and that will make it difficult for you to establish and maintain your boundaries. And when people make the assumption that you are a pushover or too nice to say anything, they're more likely to take advantage of you (intentionally or unintentionally).

In this chapter, my hope is to provide you with resources to better support you when it's time to have those uncomfortable conversations. I once heard someone say, "Courage is fear that says its prayers." It takes courage to do things that scare us.

We All Have to Have Them

Even as an adult, having tough conversations isn't easy. Sometimes I still wish I didn't have to have them, but I do.

Recently, I was booked for a speaking engagement. The speech that I was supposed to give was originally in person, but it got shifted to a virtual event. When we agreed that I would come speak they had a budget to pay me ten thousand dollars. Once they made the decision to go online, they said their budget had significantly changed and they could now only pay me two thousand dollars.

As you know, math has never been my strong suit, but I knew that math didn't add up. They were still asking me to perform the same job, regardless of the event being in person or not. I remembered that someone I knew casually had recently spoken there—let's call her Jenny—and that she'd done her talk online. Something inside of me said I should reach out to her and see if I could get some additional information about her experience and fee.

Now, let me pause. This is a type of conversation I had never had before. I was legit about to ask some lady I kind of knew if she would be comfortable talking to me about how much an organization had paid her. But just like I've told you in other chapters, if we don't advocate for ourselves, who else will?

My curiosity about whether I was being compensated fairly was larger than my fear of the uncomfortable conversation. Because if I didn't get more info, I would always be wondering if that organization tried to play me. I was also very concerned about the idea that I might not be receiving fair compensation. I mean, come on, my life's work is to make the job site better for Black and brown women, and that includes myself.

I took the leap and reached out to Jenny. I told her that I would be speaking at the same company she just spoke at and that I thought they might not be paying me what they were paying other speakers. I said I hated to put her in this position, but would she feel comfortable telling me what they offered her?

Jenny was very cool about it. She told me that they were paying her nearly my originally stated amount and they were buying her book in bulk for the attendees. With this new information, I was disappointed in the organization, of course, but I was also happy that I'd done my research. I then had to decide if I was going to have another tough conversation—this time with the organizers of the event.

As I've said, each of these conversations was completely out of my comfort zone. But I knew I had to have them!

After I gathered all the information, I sat and thought about what I wanted to say to the organizers. I knew that I couldn't go back to them and say, "Jenny said blah blah blah." Jenny was kind enough to be honest with me, and I didn't want her decision to share information with me to affect her relationship with the organization. Additionally, I didn't want to have the conversation with the organizers while I was upset. So I gave myself a couple of hours to figure out what I wanted to say.

Your Approach

Before I tell you how the conversation went, I want to talk about how I processed my thoughts and planned for the conversation.

I thought about three things: emotion, perception, and openness. Let's break each of these ideas down a little bit more.

Emotion. This company was choosing to pay me, a Black woman, less than what they were offering a white woman to do the same type of work. I had every right to be disappointed and upset.

At first, I wanted to say forget it, I don't want to do the speaking engagement at all. My mind went to this negative place, where they were trying to treat me poorly because I am a Black woman. I went down the rabbit hole that sometimes we go down, because it feels good to feel your anger for a bit. I knew I couldn't have that tough conversation with the event organizers yet. I needed to let myself feel those feelings so that I could remain professional when I did eventually speak to them.

I am a public speaker and that is part of my job. If I handled this situation the wrong way, meaning getting upset or making assumptions, that might get out to future potential clients who want to hire me. And when you are considering having a tough conversation, I would encourage you to consider all the possible outcomes.

Perception. How was I interpreting this situation? What was my perception of it? Could I imagine what the company's perception of the situation might be?

My initial perception was that they were trying to cheat me. But then I told myself to think about it some more. Could there be some other reason why they didn't offer me what they offered Jenny? Maybe they were trying to cheat me, but maybe they weren't. I can't and won't make excuses for them, but I had to allow myself to look at my situation from various perspectives.

Some might call what they were doing unconscious bias or an unchecked bias by offering me a lower fee. I began to think about what the change in speaker fee could be if it wasn't something negative. Maybe their financial situation had changed in a way that would affect all future speakers. I would need to have a tough conversation to find out.

Openness. If I was going to be a big girl and have this tough conversation, then I also had to be open to hearing what the organizers had to say.

That's another part of the reason I needed to sit with my emotions: The only way to get to an open mindset was to process my feelings first. I had to decide even before I initiated this conversation if I would be willing to be open and hear the full story. It wouldn't serve me at all to just say what I had to say and then end the conversation.

Have you ever been in a tough conversation and had the

other person just hang up the phone on you or never respond to what you've said to them? That person never wanted to have a real conversation. A real conversation happens on both sides.

I didn't want to have a "gotcha" moment with these people. I wanted to come to an understanding and find a way to work together—or, if that didn't work out, I wanted them to know where I stood and why I needed to walk away. I won't make up some fantasy that everyone will smile and listen, and no emotions will flare up, but we can be open to hearing from one another.

I Won't Leave You Hanging

I know you're probably thinking, come on, Minda, what ended up happening?

I have to tell you, this was probably one of the harder conversations I've had in a long time. And I am so happy I had it, because it has helped with my confidence and growth as a communicator. If I'm honest with you, I still can't believe I went through with it. But I knew I had to advocate for myself, otherwise I would be sad and left only with my emotions and perceptions.

I know the suspense is killing you, but let me walk you through how I decided to approach this conversation. Over the years, I've created a framework called the Seven-Step process, which has helped me start and continue difficult conversations. Now, seven might seem like a lot of steps, but even trying just one or two of the steps may help you feel more prepared.

Having tough conversations doesn't come naturally for me, so I had to find my happy place to help me lean into my courage. And I hope that you can find some peace and support the next time you have to have a difficult conversation! You can always start by playing one of your favorite songs to help hype you up, and then lean into these next seven steps.

Bet on yourself. Having tough conversations with people from your parents to crushes to your first manager is never easy. I haven't found it easier knowing the person or not knowing them. I would prefer to never have tough conversations if I had a choice, but it isn't healthy to throw the covers over your head and pretend that issues will go away just because you choose not to confront them.

In this case, I was nervous to reach back out to the organizers, but I knew I deserved to understand why I was being paid less than another speaker. And I needed to bet on myself because self-advocacy is part of loving yourself. I made a choice and chose me!

Encourage yourself. I had to encourage myself that I was doing the right thing by having this conversation—even as the little voice inside my head was trying to persuade me to just leave it alone. I thought about my purpose and why I started my company, The Memo LLC, in the first place. My goal was to help create more equality for women and girls that look like us. If I took this speaking opportunity for less than I was worth, I could be helping to widen that wage gap I told you about earlier.

Advocating for myself was advocating for all Black and brown women, who deserve to be paid fairly. I ended up playing my favorite Beyoncé song and forged ahead by reminding myself that I am worth it and so are you! And if you don't have any other people around at the time, encouraging yourself can go a long way.

You have the information. This is one of the most important steps. When you're considering having a tough conversation, gather your receipts first. Don't just start popping off about your point of view without having all of the details.

It would have been easy for me to try to argue with the organizers when I originally felt like they were being unfair by not paying me what we agreed to. But in order to have a stronger case, I needed some evidence that would support my stance. And Jenny was able to help fill in those gaps with new information.

Onward. This is also important: If you feel strongly about having this conversation, don't talk yourself out of it. I will be honest with you and say that at this stage, I definitely was thinking about just letting it go, but I decided to move forward due to my values, principles, and boundaries.

Navigate your emotions. I also knew that I needed to handle this situation professionally, because this organization was heavily connected to potential clients that might hire me in the future, and if I chose to act like a jerk about it, then that wouldn't help us get to a resolution. I wanted to remain professional and not emotional. We can say what we need to say and still keep it cute!

Concrete facts. You already have the information—now you need to stick to those facts during the conversation. I had to remember when speaking with this company that I wanted to be able to come to a resolution, or at least an understanding. And that meant that I couldn't make assumptions or point any fingers.

I just needed to keep my conversation rooted in what I knew my truth to be. And that truth was that I could not, in good faith, talk about how to make the workplace better for women of color and not be compensated fairly. If they were able to offer a fair price, I would love to work together. I gave them my facts and they had an opening to give me their truths and facts as well.

End it. I've mentioned that we can only control what is within our control. I was able to control whether or not I would have this conversation. And, after having it, I couldn't go back and forth in my mind about the possible outcomes. I had to own it, end it, and hope for the best.

Ending it means letting go once the conversation wraps up. Regardless of the outcome, you did it! In this case, I felt so much better after advocating for myself and the future women of color they hire.

Okay, now the moment you've been waiting for—what happened?

I had the conversation and the outcome was positive. I told the organizers how I was feeling about the new fee they proposed. I said that I was concerned that they were asking me to do the same work that they originally offered me ten thousand dollars for, but with a heavily decreased rate of two thousand dollars.

I let them know that, after speaking with others who had worked with them (not mentioning Jenny by name!), I had learned that what they were offering me wasn't aligned with their usual rates. I reminded them that I was a bestselling author, and that my book, *The Memo,* was very popular. I told them that I would be very happy to speak to their organization, but that they would need to pay me the ten-thousand-dollar fee we'd originally agreed to. And they said yes!

Look at that! I mean, listen, what if I never had that conversation? Because I did it, I got to do the job and get paid fairly for it. I agonized over it—it's a struggle every time I have to have a tough conversation, and sometimes they don't go my way. But advocating for myself worked out this time!

A Lesson Learned

Before we move on, I want to tell you an important lesson I learned about myself and my preferred communication style after reflecting on difficult conversations I've had over the years.

It's important to understand how we can best engage and feel our most authentic selves during a hard conversation. For example, I believe the reason the tough conversation went well with the event organizers was because I remained calm, respectful, and entered the conversation not trying to battle, but to truly come to an understanding. Even if that understanding meant we weren't able to work together at this time.

I have found that I am able to have the most productive conversations when others meet me with similar intentions and respect. I hope you will start to think about what your style is as well, as you continue reading or listening to this chapter.

Quick Q's: What words would you use to describe your communication style? How do you like people to approach you with tough conversations, and how can you show this same courtesy to others?

Girls Like You

Recently, I had the opportunity to connect with an amazing group of Black and brown young women ages fourteen through twenty in the state of Indiana.

I asked each of them about their experiences with having hard conversations at school, home, or work. Many of the girls said they would prefer not to have tough conversations if they didn't have to.

Then one of the girls made a comment during our discussion that has played in my head on a loop ever since. Destiny said, "Hard conversations genuinely allow you to see who somebody is." She explained that she went to a high school where she didn't always feel seen, as a Black student in a predominantly white student body. Destiny quickly learned that she had to push herself to have tough conversations. Without those conversations, she would never get the outcomes she wanted at school.

I was intrigued by how Destiny was able to lean into her courage and center herself during these uncomfortable conversations, despite what others might think. I asked Destiny a follow-up question: How was she able to push past her own perception that others might think she was "too angry" or "difficult" when she spoke up?

She said, "Honestly, I embrace it. I would be doing a disservice to myself if I didn't speak on things that are important to me. Especially when those things mean more to me than how someone else feels about me." When Destiny made that follow-up statement, I could tell that she inspired many of the other girls in that virtual roundtable discussion.

Destiny's comments led to a larger discussion around the anxiety that some of the other girls felt about their white classmates or teachers seeing them as the "angry Black woman."

As we dug a little deeper into their lived experiences and how some white people had demonized them for standing up for themselves, another one of the girls chimed in.

Trinity said that having tough conversations with white people is difficult because she's often met with defensiveness. She tries to remain as calm as possible so no one can try to call her angry, but she admitted these types of conversations can be triggering for her. Trinity later explained, "When a person really wants to grasp a concept or understand what you're going through, the conversation runs smoothly, but if they just want to be heard, or they already think that you're wrong—it's a very hard conversation to have, and those are hard conversations I don't like having."

I could hear the frustration in the girls' voices when they spoke about tough conversations with white peers or teachers. They talked about how they didn't feel heard or seen, especially when they were in majority white spaces. It can be hard enough having tough conversations regardless of the topic, but they felt like race further complicates the conversation and makes them not want to engage at all. I let them know that is a normal feeling.

As we talked about how race makes tough conversations harder, another participant in the roundtable brought up her experience in a seminar she was taking on anti-racism. Imani said that she doesn't avoid tough conversations, but she isn't always the first one to bring them up. Just like Destiny, Imani had learned to push herself to speak up when she felt that her classmates had said something racially offensive. Her professor encouraged all the students in the seminar to establish their own boundaries, and told them that everything couldn't be solved by agreeing to disagree. Sometimes you have to talk things out so you can understand others' perspectives and show them where you stand.

Since Imani started taking this course, she has found that she likes helping to educate her classmates on matters they have no lived experience around. She is also starting to use social media to help her speak out more on topics that might be uncomfortable in person. Imani said, "It's okay to make people uncomfortable, that's how you grow. You're not going to grow if you stay in the same place." I couldn't agree more. The only way we will be able to have the conversations that we need to have is by pushing ourselves and practicing.

For some people, speaking up about hard truths comes easy. Others might need to practice what they want to say, or write down some notes before having a tough conversation. The author, comedian, and actress Amanda Seales once said, "If you can't speak it, write it." The main point is, you have a voice—you can find a way to use it!

That roundtable discussion made me think about having tough conversations around race, especially with younger white kids who don't have the range or the maturity to have complex conversations. And to be fair, some people of color don't know how to have them either.

Let me tell you about one of my own experiences on this front . . . Remember when one of my so-called friends called me a tar baby? After she said it, I didn't want to hear anything else she had to say. I was furious! I no longer wanted to be friends with her and that was that! I couldn't care less why she'd said it or how many times she apologized. She couldn't have possibly thought that it was okay to joke like that.

As a teenager, I didn't have the range to have a mature conversation with her about what she'd said. I was too hurt to see any solution other than cutting her off. I told myself that she was racist, and that she had to have heard it from someone in her family and if that was the case, I couldn't be friends with her any longer.

I vividly remember her calling me on the phone and wanting to talk about it, but I didn't want to hear anything she had to say. She tried hard, but I didn't engage at all. Later in high school, I was able to forgive her and say hello when I would see her in the hallways, but we never restored our friendship.

If I'd had the tools to have a hard conversation about race, we might have at least been able to talk about it. Often, I think about what could have happened if I'd listened to her. What if I'd heard her out?

She might have told me that she didn't know it was wrong to say, or that she'd heard someone she knew say it, and that she was very sorry. I might have told her how that word made me feel, and we could have figured things out from there together. But I never gave us that opportunity.

And if I'm being honest, there have been times when I've

been in the wrong, and I've desperately wanted the other person to choose to have the tough conversation with me so that we could hear each other out and move forward.

Quick Q's: **What have you done when one of your classmates has said something inappropriate about your hair, your name, or your race? Did you tell them what they said is not okay, or did you let it slide? What would you have done differently, knowing what you know now?**

I want you to know that your voice matters. This chapter will help you develop the tools to articulate how you're feeling instead of completely shutting down, like I did with my friend. I wish all your peers had adults who could teach them about empathy, and help them grow their awareness of how racism affects all of our lives. But that isn't always the case. Just because those kids or adults might not have the range, doesn't mean that you can't still initiate the conversation, so they know where you stand if nothing else.

I want to make sure that you always have the tools to take on a tough conversation about race. But having the tools doesn't always mean you'll have the emotional energy to engage in the moment, and it definitely doesn't mean you won't get hurt. I'll be honest with you: Those hurtful comments you hear in junior high and high school unfortunately don't stop when you get to be my age. Kids who don't understand racism become adults who don't understand racism.

But remember: You're not going into these conversations alone. Being Black or brown is a part of you just like it's a part of me, and we are perfect exactly as we are. I'll be rooting for you every step of the way.

Address It Head-On

I remember when I was a teenager and one of my brothers was in the second or third grade.

At that time, both of my brothers were growing their hair out and my mom would braid their hair. One style she gave them was braids with some fun-colored rubber bands. I remember how excited both of them were—they thought they were too cool for school.

But when my youngest brother came home after wearing those braids to school for the first time, I could see that something was wrong. He told me that one of the boys at school, Bruno, bullied him about his hair and called him names.

I was so mad! I couldn't believe someone would hurt my little brother like that. I asked him if he wanted me to give that bully a talking-to. Of course he told me no! Mainly because he didn't want his older sister going to fight his battles; and he didn't want me to make it worse. And I definitely understood his concern.

But the next day, the bullying happened again. I asked my brother more about Bruno and found out that he actually played down the street from where we lived. I knew I better not do anything that would embarrass my brother—he still had to go to school with these kids—but I'm a pretty protective older sister, and he didn't know how to advocate for himself yet. So I walked him down to where this kid Bruno was playing, and I called him over.

I asked him straight up, "Do you have a problem with my brother's hairstyle?" He looked at me like I was a crazy lady.

To be fair, Bruno was a big kid for his age, and he looked down at me while I was talking to him. He seemed to be in shock that I was even there! I proceeded to ask him if anyone had ever made fun of him, and how did that make him feel. He agreed that when people make fun of him, it makes him feel bad about himself. I ended the tough conversation with Bruno by telling him that I hoped I never had to go back there and speak with him again.

He said okay and that he was sorry. Let's just say that my brother never had any more problems out of Bruno again.

I'm sharing this story to show how important it is to address issues head-on (whether you're advocating for yourself or for someone you love). I knew I needed to address Bruno in a polite and stern way, while holding him accountable for his bullying; otherwise, Bruno might continue bullying a lot of other kids.

Now, I can't say what type of man Bruno grew up to be, and there have been other tough conversations I've had over the years that haven't gone this smoothly. But I hope our five-minute conversation helped him become less of a bully as he grew up, and it was important for my brother to learn how to advocate for himself when someone wasn't treating him right. This was a tough conversation to have, but it's one I've never regretted.

And my brother has no problem at all advocating for himself now as an adult—I'd like to think I had a little something to do with this!

Let's look at another bullying scenario. What if you were at school and one of your classmates, Jon, made the comment, "I would never want to have hair like yours, it's not pretty like Becky's hair"? Jon compared your hair to a white girl's hair. You and I both know how racism factored into what Jon said, and there's no way to avoid it. What Jon said was offensive, plain and simple.

You might have been caught off guard by Jon's comment. Maybe you didn't have time to use the Seven-Step framework that I gave you earlier inside of this quick conversation. What can you say when things like this happen in the moment that need to be addressed?

You could consider asking Jon to talk after class. And when you address him, I would say something along the lines of, "Jon, what you said about my hair today in class was rude, and I'm happy with the hair I have. Becky is happy with the hair she has too; good thing we don't all have to have the same hair. I would appreciate it if you don't speak about my hair again. Thanks, Jon."

Jon may or may not listen to you. He might even have an attitude. But didn't that just feel good to read? His reaction isn't the point; the point is how *you* feel.

The most important thing I want you to come away with

from this chapter is that you deserve to center yourself and stand up for yourself when the situation calls for it. If Jon is a good guy, he will apologize, but if he doesn't, it wasn't about receiving the apology anyway. It was about setting your boundaries.

There will always be some kid saying something they shouldn't, but you get to decide how to handle them. No one should get a laugh or think they are being funny at your expense or well-being.

What About the Adults

One last tough conversation we haven't discussed yet is when you need to have these types of conversations with your family.

Sometimes I think I've had a more difficult time addressing hard topics with family members than with strangers because I don't want to hurt their feelings or disappoint anyone. And sometimes our family members don't have the tools they need either to hear us out or engage in productive conversations, and that can make some conversations harder than they need to be.

Back in my senior year of high school, I needed to tell my parents about something that happened while I was visiting family in Texas for the summer. On my trip, I saw a family member that no one in the family engages with due to some of their toxic lifestyle choices. I didn't intend to see them, but another family member had recently started communicating with them. I felt pressured to engage, but I knew that my parents might feel some type of way when they found out I had spent time with this relative without them knowing about it up front.

When I returned to Illinois, I wanted to tell my parents about seeing this long-lost relative, but I didn't know how to approach the situation. I didn't know if they would be upset, happy, or some mix of emotions. I kept giving myself a pep talk about it. I couldn't bring myself to verbally tell them about the encounter, and I ended up writing them a note instead. I felt a little silly at the time writing the note, but I knew I needed to address the situation. I just didn't know how.

I had never had to have such an adult conversation with them, even though I wasn't an adult yet—it felt so heavy to have to bring up. And the last thing I wanted to do was hide it from them. I believe if you are honest with the people you love, it will only strengthen your relationship—even if it doesn't feel like it at the time.

After I gave my parents the note, we were able to sit down and have a conversation. My parents were a little upset, but they were mostly mad that one of my adult relatives had put me in that tough situation to begin with. At the end of the day, I am glad that I had the conversation, because it led to a larger discussion of why my parents no longer engage with that particular relative. And after meeting them, I can definitely understand why!

Sometimes hard conversations with family might include taboo topics that aren't always discussed, but it doesn't mean you can't have a dialogue in a healthy manner, when you have the tools to have those conversations. The bottom line is, if you decide to mail a letter, send an email, or call someone on the phone—find ways to have the conversation that make you feel the most comfortable.

As you are thinking about how to tackle your next tough conversation, here are six steps to keep in mind:

Ask yourself what you want to get out of having this conversation. Do you want the other person to just listen to you, to let you get this tough thing off your chest? Do you want to engage in a real dialogue and truly listen to each other's perspectives? Or do you need some support and guidance from the other person? Maybe it's a mix of all three.

In the conversation I just described with my parents, I wanted to make them aware of what had happened, and I hoped it would lead to a real dialogue about that estranged family member, which I believed was long overdue. You might start out a conversation by saying, "Hey Granny, I want to talk to you about something and I really need a good listener right now," or "Hey Mom, I've had something on my mind for a while now, and I was hoping I could get your advice about it."

What do you want to say? What are your talking points or the main themes you want to cover? For example, if you want to ask to stay overnight at a friend's house and you know your parent or guardian is not into sleepovers, think about what you might need to say to make the conversation more productive and write those points down. It will help you center your goals and organize your thoughts.

And if you have a family member that is not so easy to talk to, maybe you can plan to begin with a disclaimer. For example: "Mom, today at school something happened that I'm not proud of, and I wanted you to hear it from me. All I ask is that you please hear me out so we can find a solution together."

Your timing. I think timing is everything and more. You probably don't want to ask one of your family members to talk as they're walking through the door with groceries in hand and you can tell they had a hard day. That conversation is not going to be good at that moment for either of you.

I understand that for some topics of conversation, depending on how heavy they are, it may never feel like the right time. But I guarantee that some times will be better for communication than others.

Keep it real. This is your opportunity to be honest, open, and direct. Like I told you before, you can't control how someone else responds to you, but you can control the information you provide and how you handle it.

Don't forget to listen. After you've said what you need to say, I hope you'll be able to engage in a two-way conversation. Again, some people, even the ones we love, might not have the tools you have to engage in tough conversations. It's important for us to remember that the person we are having the conversation with might need a day or longer to process what you have told them. They might seem defensive at first, but it could be they come back to you later and want to dig deeper into the conversation. So if you can, try to give them a little grace in how the rest of the conversation goes.

What if it goes wrong? I wish I could tell you that every tough conversation that you have will go exactly how you plan. But sometimes conversations get messy and the people we decide to share with say something that hurts our feelings, or they don't allow us to be heard. If this happens, I hope it won't stop you from having those tough conversations in the future, and I hope you find comfort in knowing that you were honest, open, and up front. If you were able to do that, you win.

So many adults don't know how to have tough conversations because no one ever coached them. By just starting the conversation, you are ahead of the pack.

Tough conversations have always been—and will always be—a part of my life. As a business owner, I probably have a tough conversation at least once a week. I can't always predict how those conversations will go, and I often find myself leaning into my courage to get ready. With family and friends, the same worries come up—but in those cases, it's personal.

Sometimes difficult topics are met with love and empathy, and other times our talks just don't turn out the way I hope they will, and that hurts. I hate to admit it, but some of my relationships with family members and friends aren't as strong as they once were because they don't know how to communicate in a healthy way. Over time, I've learned who I can have certain conversations with, and who I can't.

I bet after you read that last sentence, you automatically thought about some people in your life that fall into either of those buckets. But the other lesson I've learned is that, regardless of how someone else responds during a conversation, I don't have to silence myself. The fact that they don't know how to communicate productively doesn't mean I don't deserve to be heard.

And remember, you can also make the choice not to engage someone who has a toxic personality. We have more power than we think we do in these conversations. I hope you'll recognize that power and either speak up or make the choice to walk away, not out of fear but out of self-love.

Okay, so we've discussed how tough conversations are part of life and how they'll always be required of us in some way, shape, or form. Now it's time for you to reflect on how you will lean into your courage and have the conversations that matter.

I've given you some examples and ways to think about how to approach the people in your life. I hope you'll always be heard with respect, and I hope you'll never forget that *you* get to decide which conversations you need to have and how to initiate them. Those are the parts of the conversation that you have control over.

Show Me What You're Workin' With

Now it's time for you to reflect on how you will lean into your courage and have the conversations that matter. Use this section to process and prepare for your next tough conversation.

1) When was the last time you allowed yourself to hear someone out? How did that feel and what did you learn by listening?

2) Let's say you receive an email from your teacher stating that you haven't turned in the last three assignments, but you know you turned all three of them in on time. How could you use the Seven-Step framework to help you prepare to have a conversation with your teacher about that?

3) Think about the last difficult situation that you probably should have addressed, but you didn't. If you could have a re-do, how would you handle that situation now?

4) What are some of the areas in your life that you have a hard time addressing?

5) Choose one of those areas and tell me how you will approach these tough conversations when they arise again. Feel free to use the Seven-Step framework!

CHAPTER 7

No More Imposters

When I was growing up there was this popular commercial that aired on television to encourage kids not to do drugs.

In the scene, a kid's dad confronts him with some drugs the parents found in the kid's closet. The dad is shocked and disappointed, and he asks his son where he learned to do drugs. The son says, "I learned it by watching you!"

As I started writing this chapter, I thought back to that commercial. I thought about some of the habits and behaviors we pick up because we're exposed to them, and the ones we never pick up because we don't see them modeled.

For example, during my formative years, I was one of the few Black kids in my school and in the small town I lived in. There were so many negative stereotypes about Black and brown people there. You've probably heard some of them yourself, wherever you live. And sometimes, when you're constantly exposed to the bias that some white people hold toward people of color, it can start to inform how you see yourself.

One example of this effect on my own self-perception was

the way white people defined what was deemed pretty and how it affected what I saw when I looked in the mirror. For so many years, I didn't see myself as pretty or cute. Back then pretty meant white girls with blond hair and blue eyes.

Unfortunately, I started to learn what pretty was by watching everyone make a big deal over those girls, who looked nothing like me. I started to hate that my hair couldn't get as straight as theirs. I started to hate that when I went swimming my hair would rise up on the top of my head and look crazy to everyone else. My environment was teaching me, maybe unintentionally, to question myself.

Quick Q's: Have you ever felt this type of invisible pressure? This pressure to belong and want to be "seen" like all the other girls?

If you don't have a good support system and a healthy mindset, high school can feel lonely. I know I felt a lot of loneliness when it came to dating, and in high school, there's so much pressure around who you're dating and who likes you. But while we might not be able to control our classmates' beauty standards, we sure as heck can control how we view ourselves and the narratives we choose to accept or reject!

High school can sometimes feel like one large dumpster fire. Especially during homecomings and proms.

I think those events caused some of my biggest moments of anxiety, and the girls I speak to who are in high school right now feel the same way.

When I was going to school, the white girls were the ones who won the homecoming court, and they were the same girls that all the guys wanted to wear their jerseys to our Friday night football games. Most of my friends wore someone's jersey to school on the home football game days, but I didn't because no one was interested in me in that way. And when you go through year after year after year of this conditioning, it can be hard not to believe these negative ideas and start to question yourself.

In this chapter, we are going to dig a bit deeper into having an empire state of mind and reclaiming our mental hygiene after so many years of toxic conditioning that we might not even realize has affected our self-esteem. When we're constantly questioning our social status or place in this world, we might start to experience something called imposter syndrome, which we'll talk more about in this chapter too. I'm going to help you replace your mental patterns with more kindness to yourself and dump those false narratives from people you probably won't even see again later in life.

We can learn to stop seeing ourselves through others' eyes. We can learn to see ourselves through our own eyes, through a lens of love, peace, and happiness. And most importantly, we can learn to retrain our minds to believe that we are more than magic, even on the days when we might be the only ones who believe that.

You are the only one that matters when it comes to how *you* see yourself and what you choose to tell yourself about yourself.

Pretty Hurts

Let me start by telling you that doubting ourselves never leads to a healthy mindset. It only chips away at the best pieces of ourselves. And continuous doubting will affect who you are and how you show up in the world.

It's hard to feel seen by the world when you don't look at yourself with love. Right now, this negative mindset might mean feeling invisible when you look at a homecoming court that doesn't include any girls who look like you. When you enter the workplace, it might mean feeling invisible when a company's "About Us" page has no Black or brown faces on it. But you're not invisible, and it's up to you to adopt a mindset that helps you feel seen. You can do that by leveraging the tools we'll discuss in this chapter.

Imposter syndrome is the name for all of these negative feelings. When you feel invisible or like you don't belong in a particular space, even though you have every right to be there—that's imposter syndrome. I wish I had known what imposter syndrome was at thirteen, and at fifteen, and at twenty-one. But I didn't. I had no way to articulate how I was feeling or what that feeling actually meant.

Now that I'm older, I understand what my triggers are and how to defuse those feelings when they start to pop up. So let's discuss what imposter syndrome is, when it might show up, how you unlearn some of those negative thoughts about yourself, and how to manage those triggers if imposter syndrome tries to come back.

You Gotta Go

Let me start by telling you that imposter syndrome cannot go where your life is taking you. Imposter syndrome will only slow you down and tell you stories that aren't true about yourself.

Imposter syndrome is that feeling that you don't belong. It's those times when you might ask yourself, "Why did they choose me?" It's that infamous moment when you walk into the room as the only one and decide not to add to the conversation because you've told yourself that what you have to say is stupid. All of these early, constant moments of self-doubt can dictate how we show up throughout the day and our life.

Quick Q's: Have you ever not raised your hand in class because you've told yourself your perspective doesn't matter? Have you walked into a classroom and decided to sit in the back to blend in, instead of securing your seat to be seen in the front of the class?

Coming from a low-income family, I had times when I felt ashamed because my classmates would make fun of kids they perceived as poor. That shame stayed with me as I grew up, and I often felt like a fraud in my early career.

For example, I remember vividly when my parents told me I would be receiving a free lunch card for my school lunch. I didn't think too much of it until I got to school the next day. At lunchtime, the teacher made an announcement: Kids with a free or reduced lunch card had to join a separate line from all the other kids. It looked like the walk of shame. Kids started laughing as a few walked over to the free lunch line.

Let me just pause here for a moment. No teacher should ever, ever, ever subject children to this type of exclusivity. No one should ever feel othered in a class or any other place, for that matter. And if that line business wasn't bad enough, the free and reduced lunch tickets looked different from the others. Was that even necessary? No, it wasn't, and I pray schools have found a better system of inclusion, because we all ate the same school system lunch.

Now back to my story. If my face could turn red, it certainly would have. I made the immediate decision in my mind that I was not going to get up and walk over to that free and reduced lunch line. That teacher got me confused if she thought I was going to subject myself to that ridicule in front of everyone in my class—I was already the new girl and the only Black girl in my class. No THANK YOU!

That day, I chose not to eat lunch. And when the kids asked me why I wasn't eating I said I wasn't hungry.

Unfortunately, this wasn't the first time I felt this way. It was actually the second. A few years prior, before moving to Illinois, I attended a private school for a period of time. There wasn't a lot of diversity, but in the third grade I didn't know anything about diversity. What I did know was that the school I was attending was kind of fancy.

There was a roundabout where the cars would drop all the kids off and pick them up. Our car wasn't all that nice to begin with, but then one of the back windows shattered and my dad just used a black garbage bag to cover it. I felt like the universe was punishing me. Just when I thought it couldn't get any worse, the passenger door got so janky that you couldn't even open it anymore, so I would always have to get into the car in this really funky way, coming in through the back and climbing over the seats to get to the front.

And yes, all the kids saw me do this every day because everyone got picked up and dropped off in that fancy roundabout. I was so embarrassed and felt like I didn't deserve to be there at school with these kids.

I never felt like I belonged. Maybe your situation isn't quite like mine, but I'm sure you've had a similar feeling. And maybe there were other kids in school with me that felt this way, but I had no way of knowing that back then.

Those feelings would haunt me as I grew up. I felt like I had to work twice as hard to prove to people that I belonged. Sometimes I would spend money on materialistic things that I didn't need just to prove that I could be fancy too. There was a period in high school where I used a lot of unnecessarily big words just to prove I was smart. The whole time, I was already smart—just not smart enough to get out of my own head!

I created negative thought patterns that convinced me that white people thought Black people were poor and stupid. The thoughts were based on stereotypes I heard reflected in things white people said, and I wanted to prove them wrong. In reality, I didn't have to prove anything to anyone but myself. As an adult, I had to figure out how to break those thought patterns. For me, therapy was a good way to help myself heal from some of those painful narratives and experiences.

I'm sharing all this candidly with you because I want you to know that you can heal from this mindset, too.

You Can Win the Battle

My early experiences, like the free lunch and car incidents, started to shape my thinking and it was a constant battle not to shrink back from important life experiences.

Eventually, I realized that I had to eat, and I couldn't go on a hunger strike because my tickets looked different from everyone else's. I realized I didn't have to get into the free and reduced lunch line right away, in front of the whole class. I could just wait until everyone else had gone and then I would be the last one in line.

But even though I might have been able to maneuver the

external part of the situation, I was still battling the internal. Because it's the stories that we tell ourselves about ourselves that really matter.

Let's dig a little deeper into these stories we tell ourselves.

Constantly feeling a sense of imposter syndrome is not healthy. So many of us battle with imposter syndrome without knowing how to address it or conquer it. It wasn't until way into my adulthood that I even gave myself permission to vocalize and be vulnerable with my feelings.

One of the most common topics women of color ask me about is how to deal with imposter syndrome, so I know I'm not alone in that struggle. We all need to get out of our own heads.

Maybe you aren't sure what it means to "be in your head." Remember when we talked about having an enemy state of mind versus an empire state of mind? You can choose to torment yourself with ideas on what others might be thinking about you, or you can choose to tell yourself positive things about yourself. When thoughts like: "They only choose me because I am Black," or "I am going to fail," or "I am a product of my environment" enter your mind, that is when the real work starts.

I would like you to replace those thoughts and reflect on when those negative patterns start to flare up. Here are a few examples of what you can say to replace those negative thought patterns:

- If I can make it here, I can make it anywhere
- I want to make my next move my best move
- I've worked too hard to lean out now

It takes courage to reframe a narrative that doesn't serve us in a positive way. And you have control over your mind. I hope you will choose having a healthier outlook every time!

Flashing Lights

The other aspect of imposter syndrome that I wanted to cover is understanding your triggers.

Let me give you an example of what a triggering event might look like in real life. Let's say you've built up your empire state of mind, you fully understand that you are awesome and you can't be bothered by any haters or negativity.

You're starting a new summer job and you're the only girl hired for the summer. When all the interns go to lunch, all the boys sit together, and you are left to eat lunch alone. You're already uncomfortable being the only brown girl working with ten college-aged white boys for the summer in rural North Carolina. But you keep pushing along.

One day, you overhear one of the boys in your cohort tell someone on the phone, "It's just us guys and some brown girl who they clearly only chose for diversity." And then he laughs.

What are you going to do next? Now, some of you might

want to go and tell that little boy all the way off, but you know that isn't the way we handle ignorance. This is where our internal well-being is so important. It's not about what they said; it's about how what they said made you feel.

There's a song by Lauryn Hill that goes, "How you gon' win when you ain't right within?" And Lauryn was right, this is an inside job.

I'm not telling you that these words or actions don't hurt. You're still human. But if we're not careful, a comment like the one this boy made can infiltrate our minds and distract us all day long. We might even play his words on a loop in our heads. Meanwhile, the boy has gone on with his day and has no idea the harm he has caused us. Or, in some cases, people like him do know the harm caused and they don't care.

Let's think about the ways this situation might be triggering. I'm a little older than you, so I'm acutely aware of what sets off my insecurities and disrupts my day. I have learned that I have two specific trigger areas:

Being the only one. When I am the only Black person in a room full of white people, it definitely makes me a little uncomfortable.

I immediately know there will probably be some mess popping off, intentionally or unintentionally. But I can't hide or shrink myself because I don't want to be in situations like these. I am probably going to find myself in predominantly white spaces for the rest of my life, and it's better for me to know how it could affect me, rather than allowing myself to feel helpless every time.

On the flip side, just because I've experienced racism and sexism in white spaces before doesn't mean that's going to happen every time I'm the only Black person in the room. Part of having a healthy mindset is trying not to always assume the worst while staying aware of how I'm feeling.

Being asked about what university I attended. In many of the environments I've worked in, the college or university people went to gives them clout, and people treat you differently (read: better) if you went to an Ivy League or top-tier school.

Because I didn't go to those schools, I often feel that imposter syndrome pop up. I worry that some people won't take me seriously because I don't have a Harvard or Stanford affiliation.

I used to feel so out of place, and if I'm honest, sometimes even unworthy because I didn't have that "prestigious" education like many of my peers. For so long, I would not even mention my schooling. I would try to avoid any conversations that led down that road.

But part of having a healthy mindset and dismantling toxic self-loathing behavior is owning the fact that I can be proud of my unique road to "success." My path doesn't have to look like anyone else's; it worked for me, and that's what matters. I had to learn to tell myself that, and practice believing it, before I could manage that trigger.

Before I understood what my trigger areas were, I would often retreat inside my head with feelings of inadequacy and not being good enough. On the outside, people might not have been able to tell these things were affecting me, but internally it was killing me. As I learned how to manage my triggers, I understood that I could control how I internalized those experiences.

As I've said before, imposter syndrome can't go where our lives are taking us. I hope you will take the time out to figure out what your trigger areas are. Maybe reading mine made you think about some of yours. Negative self-talk only stops us from being more than magic. And honestly, if others get a whiff of some of the things that trigger you, they could even try to use them against you, and we don't want anyone to have power over us.

The example I gave about hearing one of your fellow interns call you a diversity hire is something that many adults often hear on their jobs, as if we are only hired to check a box and not because of our talent. Remember when I said some kids that demonstrate racist behavior might grow up with those same thought patterns and bring them into the workplace? I think many times those adults could have benefited from hearing why that type of language is not okay much sooner. If you know that hearing language like that is triggering, what might be a way to handle it?

We've already discussed a couple of options: 1) Address it

with your peer head-on. You can have that tough conversation that we discussed in Chapter Six, or 2) Have your affirmations handy for moments that drain you like these, so you can fill yourself back up. It's important that we reaffirm ourselves in these moments, so that these triggers don't stay triggering us all day long.

Quick Q's: Think back to experiences in which you felt like an imposter. What things did people say to you that made you doubt yourself? Are there common triggers that you can point to in each of these instances?

Time to Reset

Now that we have delved into triggers, let's talk about ways to navigate imposter syndrome when those triggers make it flare up. I'm going to walk you through some tips using my triggers so you can see how I manage them in real time.

When I told you about my two triggers, did you see a pattern? I feel triggered when I am the only Black woman in the room and when I feel othered because of my educational background. My triggers are pretty much two sides of the same coin: Whether I'm worried about being the only one or about being othered, it all boils down to being triggered by getting singled out. I'm constantly fighting to dismantle my fear of that feeling in my life, now that I understand the environments that heighten it for me.

Here are the steps I take—and that you can as well—to do this:

Mindset Shift. I am probably going to sound like a broken record here (but if you haven't figured it out by now, that's what a big sister does). Most of these feelings of insecurity are deep in our bones and in our minds. It's not to say that people haven't said or done some crappy things, but their crappy ways don't have to make us feel like crap about ourselves. You feel me?

The late rapper Nipsey Hussle said it best: "Most important thing is to get rid of doubt. If you got doubt in what you're doing it's not gonna work." If we doubt ourselves, then it's going to be hard to slay our dreams and go after what we want full out.

I am not asking you to make a commitment to me—I am asking you to make a commitment to yourself. In my case, when I find myself being the "only," I remind myself that I am more than magic and I belong here just as much as anyone else, and I don't have to shrink.

Those people we are concerned with are probably not giving us as much energy as we are giving them. I remind myself that in order to get the full experience of being on the team or at the table, I have to be present. If I'm having a mental gymnastics meet in my mind, then I'll miss out on what is meant for me in that room.

So I choose to commit to myself. I don't have to ignore reality, but I can choose a new reality—one that centers me. I choose to be right within.

It is a daily practice to choose a healthy mindset. You have the power to change your perception of the situation, even though you might never be able to change the people you interact with in those rooms.

Love All Parts of You. I love myself, always. When I'm experiencing imposter syndrome, I still love myself. Overall, I have a positive attitude about who I am. But, because of some of my early childhood experiences, there used to be pieces of myself and my life that I didn't want anyone to know about or see, and I would sometimes tie not having the Stanford degree to my self-worth.

Eventually, I started to realize that yes, those things are nice, but I'm happy with the person I've become. I have a family that loves me, I have professional success, and I get the opportunity to help others in the work that I do. What more could I ask for?

None of those successes are tied to where I went to college. When someone asks me where I got my undergrad degree from, I now proudly say, "Western Illinois University. It's a great state school in Illinois." In 2017, I was able to establish a scholarship there for Black and brown girls entering college for the first time or transferring from a community college. I wanted other young girls that look like me to have everything they needed to succeed, and I'm proud that I was able to make that happen.

Sometimes It Can Be Your Own

Because this world can be a little wild, you might encounter some folks who look like you who make you question yourself.

Have you heard the expression "All skinfolk ain't kinfolk"? This came from a similar comment made by the writer Zora Neal Hurston. People use it to talk about the times we get burned by people who look like us.

Just because someone shares your skin color doesn't always mean they want the best for you. Nastiness sees no gender, race, or age. The same rules and tips apply to anyone who makes you feel like you don't belong.

I constantly have to remind myself that I am not in competition with anyone else—my only competition is with myself. There will never be a time in your life where you don't meet other people who have more money than you or who are smarter than you in some areas, but what someone else has should never make you feel less than. If you have to, tell yourself in the morning before you get out of bed that you are enough, and say it again at lunchtime, and again before you go to bed. Say it until you truly start to believe it.

Did you know that even our former First Lady Michelle Obama talks about how she has experienced imposter syndrome? In 2019, she was named the Most Admired Woman in the World by Gallup—and even she doubts herself sometimes. Obama once said to a group of young girls, "I still feel that at some level I have something to prove because of the color of my skin, because of the shape of my body . . . who knows how people are judging me." So, you are truly not alone! But just like Michelle Obama, you don't have to let this feeling paralyze you.

Room to Grow

As you continue to be more than magic, remember to give yourself room to grow. There is no expectation for you to be perfect. My only hope is that you will commit to healthy self-talk when negative thoughts or feelings pop up.

You don't need to take this unnecessary baggage with you as you continue to conquer the world. We often carry around a lot of toxic thoughts and experiences with us, but they don't serve us, and they never will. As you grow up, begin to build adult relationships, get your first job, and find your career, remember that you can leave those negative thoughts and experiences behind.

I want to share one last example with you about a woman I met when I was on a book tour a couple of years ago. Let's call her Monica.

Monica was about twenty years old at the time and she did not have a college degree, but she had earned a certificate in software engineering from a reputable coding academy, which is a type of technical job training boot camp. After graduating from that intensive six-month program, she was hired by a very prominent company and had been working there for two years by the time I met her.

Monica was ecstatic because she was finally pursuing her goals and making an amazing salary. This new salary allowed her to move out of her parents' house and into her own apartment. Monica worked hard for what she had. But even though Monica was living her best life, she worried that she would always feel a little intimidated by her coworkers because all of them had degrees from some of the top schools in the country.

Whenever one of her coworkers asked her where she went to college, Monica always felt like she should make up a school, because she could see how their posture changed when she said she didn't have a college degree. She felt a little ashamed that she had graduated from a coding boot camp.

Now, the reality is, they were all doing the same job, regardless of their backgrounds, but Monica felt othered. She felt less than because she didn't have a college degree, and her feelings were reinforced by some of her colleagues' nonverbal communication. She constantly tried to shake off that feeling of imposter syndrome, because she was so happy with her life and new career, but she couldn't stop worrying about her colleagues judging her.

Monica had big plans to climb the corporate ladder and was very engaged at work. During a virtual staff meeting, she brought up new research she had recently read related to a product her company was developing. Her colleague Kim replied, "What do you know? You don't have a college degree."

I don't know about you, but a situation like that would upset me so much that I'd turn my camera off and leave the meeting completely. Maybe you'd have the opposite reaction: After hearing something like that, you might want to stick around and give Kim a piece of your mind. But leaving wouldn't solve the problem at hand, and neither would yelling at Kim.

Let's keep it real, what Kim did and said was out of control. And I would bet money that this wasn't the first time Kim said something hurtful in a meeting to Monica or someone else. We all know people like Kim. It's unfortunate that Kim probably showed signs of being combative as a teenager and no one put a stop to it.

Monica's goal wasn't to teach Kim a lesson—Kim's behavior is not Monica's responsibility. Instead, she had to focus on not letting Kim's bias become something that she carried around in her mind. In an ideal world, Kim and Monica's manager would have chimed in and let Kim know that her comment was inappropriate, but what tends to happen in these moments is that no one says anything and the meeting just continues on like nothing happened.

Quick Q's: Have you ever experienced something like this in one of your classes or on a team?

We won't always be able to control someone else's perception of us, but we completely control how we see ourselves. Imposter syndrome makes us question ourselves, and we can no longer allow it to do that.

In Monica's case, she had to learn to own her place in this world. There will always be people like Kim that we come across, but they shouldn't be able to make us feel bad about ourselves and our unique paths. Monica was able to obtain a certificate in six months and others might have had to attend a four-year university to get hired, but at the end of the day, they are working at the same place. Does it matter how they got there?

Monica has the opportunity to grow in her career. The people that hired her knew her qualifications, and she deserves to be there just like her coworkers. The good news is, Monica's manager noticed this toxic behavior coming from Kim, and gave her a verbal warning, because that isn't the type of dynamics he wants on his team. And because Monica's manager had a difficult conversation with Kim, her behavior changed going forward and Monica could thrive in her role.

Black and brown girls: people will always try to question our place in the world. That's *their* problem. We don't have to join them. We have a place and we each get to decide what that looks like and position ourselves accordingly!

Your Pieces Belong to You

When I look back on my decisions early on with the lunch tickets or feeling some kind of way because I didn't go to an Ivy League school, I have a different perspective now. I am more informed and understand the nuance (a difference in meaning or expression) of life better than I did at that age.

I have learned to love myself. I have learned to love ALL the pieces of myself. The pieces that were part of the working poor when I was younger, the pieces that used food stamps, the pieces that had a loving family, and the pieces that made me become a bestselling author. I would never have become the woman I am today without all of those pieces.

Once you start to love all the pieces of you, you will no longer try to pray for different pieces, because you'll know that those pieces make you who you are.

I hope you will learn early on that you can't let others shape your identity. Your identity belongs to you. In the example I gave earlier about Monica and Kim, Kim attempted to try to shape or influence Monica's identity by assuming that she wasn't as smart as everyone else because she didn't go to college. That is Kim's issue, but it doesn't have to be Monica's. And if Monica knows that conversations about college are a trigger area for her, then she will have to work a little harder not to play into that.

Zooming out, some white people who have never had a real relationship with a person of color might view us as too loud, too aggressive, and all those other negative stereotypes. That's their issue, but it doesn't have to be ours.

The first Latina woman appointed to the United States Supreme Court, Justice Sonia Sotomayor, once said, "I do know one thing about me: I don't measure myself by others or let others define my worth." It starts in our own minds. We must have such a high measure of ourselves that despite what someone else says or does it holds no bearing on who we actually are.

We certainly can't live our lives trying to fit into other

people's boxes and we can't box ourselves in with our own negative thoughts. I will say it again, for the people in the back: Imposter syndrome can't go where you are headed. You have colleges to choose from, you have sports teams to try out for, and you have new jobs to slay. The only thing I want you to focus on is doing your best and practicing each and every day to have a healthier mindset.

I hope you will continue to have an empire state of mind no matter what, because you don't need to be an enemy of your own growth and development.

Show Me What You're Workin' With

Now it's time to reflect on how you see yourself. I've given you some things to consider around building a healthier mindset. Use this section to reflect and help beat any imposter syndrome that might try to hold you back.

1) When was the last time that you experienced imposter syndrome?
2) What situations trigger your imposter syndrome?
3) What action steps will you commit to the next time imposter syndrome flares up?
4) What advice would you give Monica if her imposter syndrome tries to show up again?

CHAPTER 8

Never Can Say Goodbye

Let me first give you a high five. You made it to the end of *You Are More Than Magic*.

As I said before, this book was written especially for you. I didn't have a book like this at your age, but now you do, and you get to let your friends know they are more than magic too—so make sure you share it with them.

I hope you'll always lean into your courage and advocate for yourself. I hope you'll remember that having healthy friendships and building a strong network will help you get where you're going in life. You deserve a squad of people that are invested in your success and your happiness.

Thank you for trusting me and joining me on this journey. I know we dug pretty deep in some of the chapters, but I hope you were able to have some laughs along the way too. And just because we're at the end of the book, it doesn't mean I stop serving as your big sister—I'm still here, and I'll always be rooting for you.

I hope you will stay connected and let me know how the rest

of your school year goes. My goal in each chapter was to remind you how awesome you are, and don't let anyone tell you any different.

Just so you know, I added some resources for your teachers and caregivers, so they can support you in the ways you might need it most. You can find them in the next section. I hope the discussion questions that I included for them will help you continue to have those difficult conversations we talked about.

Lastly, always remember that you have the power to create a life that makes you feel happy, empowered, and seen!

Show Me What You're Workin' With

And just like I ended all the other chapters, I can't leave you without a few things to consider . . .

1) What were your favorite chapters in this book? Why?
2) If you could add more chapters to this book, what would you want them to address?
3) Did you find it hard to answer the questions I posed at the end of each chapter in an honest way? Why?
4) How did this book help change the way you view yourself and your place in this world?
5) What does it mean to you to be more than magic?

For Caregivers and Educators
of Girls of Color

My hope is that if you are reading this book and you're an adult in the lives of these young women, they will have your full support to continue showing up in the world as more than magic.

The support they might need includes hearing them out when they build up the courage to have a tough conversation with you. I hope your support will include challenging them to be their best selves. And most importantly, when the world tries to make them a hidden figure, I hope your support won't allow them to feel that way in their classes, their homes, or on their first jobs.

I don't know about you, but I wish I'd had a guide to remind me that I was more than magic on the days when I felt like dust. As a young Black girl, I had some amazing moments growing up, but I also experienced moments that had me questioning my place in this world. And we can't be our best when we can't show up as our authentic selves.

Our young people are working hard to figure out who they want to show up as in their classes, on their sports teams, at their internships, and in their friendships. And as they work on investing in their futures, I want to make sure they have a team on the outside ready to step up and continue to support them.

That's why I included this chapter in the book. I am challenging you—yes, you—to help them be all that they can be.

Supporting them might require you to get some new tools in your toolkit. Situations and experiences will arise in their lives that might not be familiar to you, but you can learn how to support them there too. They are going to need you to be your best self and rise to the occasion.

You're an important part of their squad. Their success is not a solo sport!

I've included a discussion guide to help lead you through important conversations with the young women in your lives. Feel free to make it your own.

But before you start using this discussion guide, first read the entire book. I would encourage you to consider two ways to engage with it. One way is to read the book by yourself to have an understanding of what some of the young people in your life might be experiencing and how you might be able to support them. Another way to read this book is to have a book club with your more than magic young adult and read the book together.

You noticed the "Show Me What You're Workin' With" section at the end of each chapter, with questions meant to help the young reader dig deeper into how they experience the chapter's topic. In the following discussion guide, I've included questions for you to ask the reader, to help them further reflect on everything they've learned. These questions will help you create a stronger dialogue with the reader and put your finger on the pulse of the issues they might be experiencing.

You could also consider creating a More Than Magic Reading Squad. If you go to www.youaremorethanmagic.com you will find some additional resources and materials to help with this.

Discussion Guide

Chapter 1: The Big Shake-Up

1) Have you ever experienced a big shake-up in your family, with friends, or in school? How did it affect you?

2) Did you find it hard or easy to discuss this big shake-up with others? Why do you think you felt that way about the conversation? If talking about it was hard, what would have made it easier?

3) How does it make you feel to know that the author wrote this book especially for girls like you? Why do you think she thought you needed a book like this in your life?

4) What does it mean to you to be a young woman of color?

Chapter 2: More Than Magic

1) Now that you understand what self-advocacy looks like, what are some ways you can advocate for yourself?

2) What has scared you about advocating for yourself in the past? And how will you fight that feeling in the future?

3) What steps will you take when you need help advocating for yourself?

Chapter 3: Don't Stop, Get It

1) Which stories in this chapter resonated with you most? Have you ever experienced some of the losses the author described?

2) We know from this chapter that sometimes, even when we try our hardest, things don't turn out the way we planned. When that happens to you, what will you do to reassure yourself that nothing is wrong with you and that you are more than enough?

3) What do you think it means to be vulnerable? Why is vulnerability important?

Chapter 4: What About Your Friends

1) What does it mean to be a good friend?

2) Give us an example of when you've been a good friend, and an example of a time someone has been a good friend to you.

3) If you start to realize that someone you thought was a friend should no longer be in your life, how will you handle the situation?

4) Why do you deserve to have good relationships in your life? Why is having a healthy relationship and boundaries important?

Chapter 5: Let's Work

1) Have you ever had a job or internship? And if so, what did you learn about yourself from the experience?

2) Let's imagine you have a job, but it's interfering with your schoolwork. What is the best way to address the situation with your supervisor?

3) How do you think the negotiation strategies in this chapter can help you now and in the future?

Chapter 6: Tough Conversations

1) Why do you think people avoid having tough conversations?

2) Why do you think it's important to have tough conversations?

3) What would you like the adults in your life to know about your communication style when they have to come to you and have a tough conversation?

Chapter 7: No More Imposters

1) What does having a healthy mindset mean to you, and why do you think it's important?

2) How can imposter syndrome hurt the way we see ourselves?

3) What would you tell a friend who doesn't think they are good enough?

4) Who do you feel comfortable speaking with when you're experiencing imposter syndrome?

Chapter 8: Never Can Say Goodbye

1) If someone you know was thinking about reading *You Are More Than Magic*, how would you describe your experience reading this book to them in five words or less?

2) Who are some people in your life that you would like to share this book with?

3) What are your top three takeaways from this chapter and how do you plan to incorporate them into your own life?

For White Caregivers of Girls of Color

Recently, I had the opportunity to interview a group of young, Black women between the ages of eighteen and twenty years old who are currently in college, sponsored by MelanatED Leaders. MelanatED Leaders builds a powerful community of education leaders of color across Indianapolis to inspire, educate, and edify each other in leadership by retaining and developing extraordinary talent in the city for students of color. At the end of our roundtable discussion, I asked the girls what they would like white adults to know about their experiences as Black girls. We had an honest conversation about some of the painful experiences they'd had in their formative years, and how those experiences have played a role in them finding it hard, at times, to trust white children and adults. Some of their responses stuck with me:

"I am not a color, I am a person."

"I am loving and caring. I might love you way before you love me."

"At the end of the day, we are all the same."

"We should be valued as a person no matter our socioeconomic status or background."

"Give us a chance. Often I feel like we never get the benefit of the doubt. Have a conversation with me. You won't know anything about me by just knowing my name or seeing my face."

"Please have more empathy and look at me like you see your daughters. I would love for you to have the same care for me like you have for your own."

"Educate yourself, and learn to dismantle your biases and stereotypes about young Black and brown girls."

"Being color-blind might sound nice, but I want you to see my color and respect it."

At this same event, I had the opportunity to interview Black high school girls who are part of a group called Dear Queens. This group was created because there aren't a lot of Black girls that attend their high school, and this was a way to provide cover and resources, and to amplify their experiences in a predominantly white high school. I'm so happy they have this group to build community and feel supported.

During my roundtable discussions with the high school girls, one major theme was the empathy gap they feel between themselves and their white classmates. They vulnerably shared stories about times they'd been mistreated by these classmates. Whether the white kids' actions were intentional or unintentional didn't matter; the result—that these girls of color were hurt—was the same.

And if we adults are not well-versed in racial dynamics, then we do our children a disservice when we show them how to engage with others.

I believe it's important to start these conversations early, so all children can apply empathy, courage, and respect to their actions. I encourage you to read this book with the young people in your life that you want to see become more racially competent and respectful of their peers from the classroom to the sports field to their first jobs working together.

You might find some of these conversations tough, but I hope you will also find them impactful and necessary. We can educate ourselves together!

If you are a white caregiver of a child who identifies as Black or brown, please be sensitive to the unique experiences and challenges they face as they move through adolescence. Please don't discount their need to feel seen even in their own home. I would encourage you to celebrate historical figures, watch movies, and attend cultural gatherings so their experiences are not constantly through the white gaze. This is a great opportunity for representation to matter inside of your home—and for you to model what diversity and inclusion *should* look like.

Buy them books that make them feel like they are more than magic. Talk to them about what it's like to be them. Too many times, I've seen white caregivers try to raise their Black and brown children to "not see race," and that only hurts them in a world that tends to see race first.

Lastly, I've added questions that can help you talk about the ideas in this book with the white kids in your lives. These conversations will help them build stronger and more equitable friendships with kids of color.

Questions for White Readers

1) Why do you think we are reading a book about young girls of color?

2) How do you think this book will help you be a better friend, classmate, or coworker to girls who might not look like you?

3) What do you think it's like to be a young Black or brown girl growing up in the world today? And why?

4) How did it feel to read the author's experience when she was the only Black girl moving to a small town with kids who didn't look like her?

5) Have you ever experienced someone mistreating Black and brown girls? How did that make you feel, and what did you do? What do you think white kids need to learn so that they can help in those situations?

6) What steps would you take if you weren't able to advocate for someone who was experiencing racism or unjust treatment, but you feel like you don't have the courage right now to address it yourself?

7) Tell me about your current friend group. Is it diverse? What is the benefit of having a friend group with people of different races in it?

8) What do you think should be done about the unequal playing field in the workplace?
9) Why do you think it's hard to have conversations around race?
10) Imagine that one of your classmates points out that something you did was racist. How would that make you feel? What would you do next? How would you hear them out, even if you meant no harm?

Additional Resources

Dear Black Girl: Letters From Your Sisters on Stepping into Your Power by Tamara Winfrey Harris

Stamped: Racism, Antiracism, and You: A Remix of the National Book Award-winning Stamped from the Beginning by Jason Reynolds and Ibram X. Kendi

Black Girls Rock!: Owning Our Magic. Rocking Our Truth. by Beverly Bond

Young, Gifted and Black: Meet 52 Black Heroes from Past and Present by Jamia Wilson

Hair Love by Matthew A. Cherry

Acknowledgments

I would like to thank God for the opportunity to serve my community with my voice via writing. To my family and friends—thank you for always praying for me, hyping me up, and rooting me on.

Thank you to Monica Odom, Dana Chidiac, Rosie Ahmed, and the entire team at Penguin Young Readers. Thank you for allowing me to push the needle forward for girls who the world may not always "see."

Thank you to my teachers in grade school, high school, and college—many of you made a mark on my life. Coaches and childhood friends that I speak to all the time, and those I haven't spoken to in years: you also helped me learn some valuable lessons along the way.

I want to give a special shout out to the girls from Indiana who shared so vulnerably with me about their experiences, and to Penny Gregory for helping me amplify their voices.

To anyone who purchased or read this book—you are now part of my squad—many thanks! And to Boston, Mommy loves you. XO